Think Tank Diplomacy

Diplomacy and Foreign Policy

Volumes published in this Brill Research Perspectives title are listed at *brill.com/rpdf*

Think Tank Diplomacy

By

Melissa Conley Tyler
Rhea Matthews
Emma Brockhurst

TUTA SUB AEGIDE PALLAS · 1683 ·

BRILL

LEIDEN | BOSTON

Originally published as Volume 2.3 (2017), in *Brill Research Perspectives in Diplomacy and Foreign Policy*, DOI 10.1163/24056006-12340007.

Library of Congress Control Number: 2017953903

Typeface for the Latin, Greek, and Cyrillic scripts: "Brill". See and download: brill.com/brill-typeface.

ISBN 978-90-04-33120-4 (paperback)
ISBN 978-90-04-33121-1 (e-book)

This book is printed on acid-free paper and produced in a sustainable manner.

Contents

Think Tank Diplomacy

Melissa Conley Tyler, Rhea Matthews** and Emma Brockhurst***

Abstract

Think tanks demonstrably play a role in diplomacy. Not long ago, the idea of think tank diplomacy would have provoked scepticism, but the nature of diplomacy has changed from a state-centric club to a polylateral network characterised by a diversity of actors and communication methods. As organisations producing independent intellectual outputs to influence public policy, think tanks engage in at least four diplomatic functions: negotiation, communication, information-gathering and promoting friendly relations in international affairs. Case studies show that think tanks both directly perform diplomatic functions and act indirectly as facilitators of diplomacy: as metaphorical hired guns, charm offensive, witnesses and safe space; as a school for diplomats, personal trainers, chief knowledge officer and wise council. Think tanks need to overcome obstacles including resource constraints and relationships with policy-makers to reach their full potential in contributing to diplomacy.

Keywords

diplomacy – think tanks – civil society – public diplomacy – public policy

Introduction

On 15 December 2016, the Center for Strategic and International Studies' Asia Maritime Transparency Initiative published photographs suggesting that China had installed weapons on seven disputed islands in the South China Sea. The satellite images were featured in CNN, BBC, *The Wall Street Journal*, *Financial*

* *National Executive Director, Australian Institute of International Affairs. Corresponding author. ceo@internationalaffairs.org.au @MConleyTyler.*

** *Former researchers, Australian Institute of International Affairs.*

 | DOI 10.1163/9789004331211_002

Times, Al Jazeera and many other news outlets around the world,[1] forcing the Chinese Foreign Ministry spokesperson to issue a response saying that China's deployment of defensive facilities was legitimate and normal (Xinhua 2016). CSIS' earlier release of images of land reclamation, memorably described as China's "great wall of sand" by US Pacific Fleet Commander Admiral Harry Harris (Schreer 2015), had successfully raised international awareness of what had been a lower-profile territorial dispute but which Germany's Chancellor Angela Merkel began to describe as a "serious conflict" (Rinke 2015).

Also on 15 December, the International Crisis Group released a report on a new Muslim insurgency in Myanmar led by emigres with links to Saudi Arabia, Pakistan and Afghanistan. It received significant coverage, from the *Los Angeles Times* to *Euronews*,[2] and generated fears that Myanmar's Rakhine state could become the next recruiting ground for Islamic State of Iraq and the Levant (ISIL) (Black 2016). A few days later foreign ministers from the Association of Southeast Asian Nations (ASEAN) met in Yangon and discussed the situation, in a rare departure from ASEAN's usual policy of not interfering in other countries' affairs. Under pressure, Myanmar agreed to grant "necessary humanitarian access" to the area (Cochrane 2016).

And in Aleppo, 15 December 2016 saw the evacuation of thousands of civilians following a ceasefire brokered by Russia and Turkey between the parties in Syria's civil war. One of these parties, Syria's High Negotiations Committee, is working with Independent Diplomat, a non-profit advisory group that supports it in diplomatic negotiations. Coverage of the evacuation relied on the work of various think tanks tracking the devastation wrought by the conflict: the UK-based Syrian Human Rights Observatory (Domonoske & Katkov 2016), the Aleppo Project at the Budapest-based Centre for Conflict, Negotiation and Recovery (Al Jazeera 2016b) and the Syrian start-up Syrian Centre for Policy Research[3] (World Breaking News 2016). At the meeting of the European Council on 15 December, the EU's 28 leaders strongly condemned the continued assault on Aleppo by the Syrian regime and its allies (European Council 2016).

1 Images available on the Asia Maritime Transparency Initiative's Island Tracker feature (Center for Strategic & International Studies 2016). Coverage includes Al Jazeera 2016a, BBC 2016, Bland 2016, Brunnstrom 2016, Hunt 2016, Lourdes Viray 2016, Page 2016, Phillips 2016b and Wroe 2016.

2 International Crisis Group 2016a. Coverage includes AFP 2016, Agrawal 2017, Black 2016, Cochrane 2016, Hackwill 2016, Kantar 2017, Lewis 2016, Murdoch 2016, McKinley Corbo 2017, Poole 2017 and a United Nations report: Office of the High Commissioner for Human Rights 2017.

3 See Fielding-Smith 2014 and http://scpr-syria.org/.

Drawn from just one day in an eventful year, these examples give a taste of the roles that think tanks can play in international affairs and the potential influence they can wield. If you start looking, you can see think tanks everywhere in international relations: from the influence of think tank studies supporting the "Leave" case in the Brexit referendum (Wright 2016) to the involvement of think tanks in negotiation of the Paris Agreement on climate change (Jacobs 2016); from the Shangri-La Dialogue to the World Economic Forum.

This latest in *Brill Research Perspectives in Diplomacy and Foreign Policy* tackles the issue of whether think tanks are involved in diplomacy. This includes questions like: Are think tanks diplomatic actors? If so, what is their role in diplomacy? How and when do think tanks perform diplomatic functions? Could their practice be improved?

It is fair to say that these are questions that have not previously received in-depth treatment.

While the literature on diplomacy is vast, including its history, definitions and practice[4]—as is the research on think tanks and their contribution to policymaking[5]—there has been little effort to bring these two areas together and consider whether think tanks have a role *in* diplomacy and, if they do, what that role might be.

For example, neither of the major handbooks on diplomacy provide a guide: you will not find a treatment of "think tank diplomacy" in the 49 chapters of *The Oxford Handbook of Modern Diplomacy* nor the 52 chapters of *The SAGE*

---

4 Resources include a dictionary of diplomacy (Berridge and Lloyd 2012); study of its etymology (Leira 2016); histories of diplomacy (Anderson 1993, Kissinger 1994, Black 2011, Cohen 2013, Zhao 2013); textbooks for teaching and learning diplomacy (Rana 2011; Kerr & Wiseman 2012); debates on the evolution and functions of diplomacy (Sofer 1988, Sharp 1997, Hocking 1999, Cooper & Hocking 2000, Bull 2002, Hocking 2004, Jönsson & Hall 2005, Langhorne 2005, Heine 2008, Neumann 2008; Leguey-Feilleux 2009, Copeland 2009, Hall 2010, Kelley 2010, Khanna 2011, Sending et al. 2011, Stein 2011, Hocking et al. 2012, Seib 2012, Heine 2013, Hocking et al. 2013, Malone 2013, Weisbrode 2014); analysis of different types of diplomacy (Montville 2009, Cooper & Frechette 2008, Melissen 2013a and 2013b, Bjola and Holmes 2015, Jones 2015, Conley Tyler and Ramasubramanian 2015, Sandre 2015, Bjola and Murray 2016, Conley Tyler & Beyerinck 2016); anthropological studies of diplomats at work and/or country studies (Renaud 2011, Neumann 2012, Cooper 2015, Byrne et al. 2016); analyses of diversity and diplomacy (Conley Tyler et al. 2014, Conley Tyler 2016); a large number of memoirs (a favourite is Woolcott 2007); and career guides for those considering a diplomatic career (Dorman 2011, Kopp and Gillespie 2011).

5 See, for example, Smith 1991, Higgott & Stone 1994, Stone 1996, Stone et al. 2004, Shambaugh 2002, Parmar 2004, Stone & Denham 2004, Rich 2005, Abelson 2006, McGann 2007, Stone 2007, Gyngell 2008, Abelson 2009a and 2009b, Abelson 2014, Conley Tyler 2015a 2015b 2015c, McGann 2015, Conley Tyler 2016.

Handbook of Diplomacy (and neither include "think tanks" in their index). Google Scholar only finds four articles in total that have ever used the phrase "think tank diplomacy";[6] in none of these is it the focus of the article. There is no Wikipedia page for "think tank diplomacy".

But if you look closer, think tanks are present in discussions of diplomatic practice: in *The Oxford Handbook of Diplomacy*'s discussions of civil society and diplomacy (Hochstetler 2013), human rights (Forsythe 2013), landmines (English 2013) and others; in *The SAGE Handbook of Diplomacy*'s chapters on citizen diplomacy (Conley Tyler and Beyerinck 2016), diplomatic mediation (Aggestam 2016) or diplomatic agency (Adler-Nissen 2016). A Google search shows the idea of think tanks being involved in diplomacy comes up in places as diverse as China, India, Ukraine, Azerbaijan, Morocco and the USA.[7]

The aim of this work is to focus on think tanks as contributors and potential actors in diplomacy on the basis that their role deserves further investigation.

This article explores how think tanks are involved in diplomacy and in what ways they contribute to diplomacy. It investigates cases where think tanks *directly* perform diplomatic functions and where they act *indirectly* as facilitators of diplomacy.

It argues that think tanks do have a role in diplomacy, not only in supporting diplomatic activity but playing roles in diplomacy in their own right. Think tanks should be recognised for their contribution to the evolving meaning of diplomacy through their work creating transnational linkages and influencing audiences both domestically and internationally.

The Changing Nature of Diplomacy

Not long ago, the very term "think tank diplomacy" would have been met with a deep scepticism or, at best, bemusement. It would have been unimaginable for organisations such as think tanks to be put in the same breath as the state-sanctioned diplomat who is accorded all the protections of the Vienna Convention on Diplomatic Relations 1961 and is the "custodian of the idea of international society" (Bull 1977: 176).

However, diplomacy has evolved so that it is no longer the preserve of the few but of the many. While official diplomats are still the primary agents in diplomacy, the diplomatic community now includes a variety of actors (Heine

6 Yang, Chen and Poong 2015, Song 2014, Tsai 2012, Jayaram 2012.

7 China: Wang 2013, Ying 2015; India: Patil 2015, Chemarapally 2016; Ukraine: Ukrainian Think Tank Liaison Office in Brussels 2016; Azerbaijan: Aslanov 2010; Morocco: Morocco World News 2012; USA: Walsh 2011.

2013: 60–63; Adler-Nissen 2016). It can be argued that these new actors—which include non-governmental organisations (NGOs), think tanks, charitable groups and even celebrities (Frechette 2013, Wheeler 2016)—are performing some of the functions of traditional diplomacy in both the activities that they undertake and methods that they utilise.

The emergence of new actors in diplomacy is indicative that diplomacy has transformed from a rigid institution in the traditional sense to what can be now characterised as a behaviour (Kelley 2010: 286). With this understanding of diplomacy as a social practice involving various diplomatic functions, the notion of think tank diplomacy is not impossible.

Method and Structure

To explore the ways that think tanks are involved in diplomacy, this paper draws upon our definition of four functions of diplomacy—negotiation, communication, information-gathering and promoting friendly relations—and looks at ways in which think tanks directly perform or indirectly facilitate these activities.

Examples have been identified where think tanks perform all of these functions of diplomacy in some way. Whether it be directly through their public diplomacy efforts, field research and second track dialogues on the one hand or, indirectly, their advice to governments, diplomatic training and policy inputs on the other, think tanks are playing roles which can be characterised as diplomatic ones.

The case study method is employed to focus in-depth on the mission and activities of a variety of think tanks of different types and selected from different geographic regions. By drawing on a broad and varied sample of think tanks, the diversity of think tanks and their roles in diplomacy can be highlighted. The use of case studies enables analysis of the successes and failures of think tanks in diplomacy to provide ideas for development and encourage further discussion.

The first section explains what think tanks are and gives a sense of the think tank landscape. It outlines the core definition of a think tank and the competing definitions of the edge of the concept. It outlines how they act as knowledge-brokers between academic research and government policy to bridge the academic-policy divide.

The second section explores the role of non-state actors and the evolution of diplomacy from a 'club' to a 'network' model. It outlines various definitions of diplomacy and outlines four diplomatic functions to be used in analysis. This generates a matrix of direct and indirect contribution to examine the potential roles for think tanks in diplomacy.

Section three builds upon this by providing case studies of the work of specific think tanks selected from a variety of regions. These case studies demonstrate that think tanks contribute both directly and indirectly to the four diplomatic functions and illustrate both the successes and challenges faced by think tanks working in the diplomatic space. A final case study of a think tank—the Australian Institute of International Affairs—illustrates how think tanks attempt in practice to perform multiple diplomatic functions.

The conclusion summarises the key findings of the article and suggests further avenues for research on this under-explored topic. It examines why think tanks may not be achieving their potential and offers some suggestions on how their contribution could be improved.

By bridging two areas—diplomacy and think tanks—this work hopes to stimulate further debate and research on a new but interesting topic of analysis. It is hoped that this will encourage think tanks and official diplomats to be more aware of each other and how they can aid in performing their functions more effectively.

Part 1. Understanding Think Tanks

Think tanks have existed for at least a century since Robert S. Brookings and his colleagues established an institute devoted to analysing public policy. Despite this long history, a working definition has lagged behind practice and there is no one commonly accepted way to define and describe think tanks. As founding director of the Lowy Institute for International Policy Allan Gyngell observes, "You now hear the expression used to describe everything from the majesty of the RAND Corporation with its 1600 staff and budget of $260 million to a couple of part-time bloggers with some strong views (Gyngell 2008: 2).

The Think Tank Landscape

Think tanks are an international phenomenon not confined to any one region. These days "the think tank is ubiquitous. The type of organisation and activity has spread into most countries" (Stone 2000: 1). While traditionally think tanks were located in the West, since the 1970s, there has been a steep rise in think tanks across the Middle East, Asia, the Asia Pacific, Latin America and Eastern and Central Europe (McGann & Weaver 2000: 4).

The growth in the number of think tanks worldwide has been spurred by the communications and technology revolution, the growing complexity of issues facing governments and the increasing presence of non-state actors in the international arena (McGann 2016: 8). It has been explained by the increased demand for think tanks by government agencies, foundations and private organisations who are looking for "high quality research, policy analysis and ideological argumentation" (Stone & Denham 2004: 1).

There is great diversity in the think tank landscape: think tanks come in many shapes and sizes, perform a range of different functions, have varied agendas and different affiliations (Conley Tyler 2015a). They can be grouped in various categories: such as academic or university, contract researchers, advocacy tanks and party think tanks (McGann & Weaver 2000: 7). To give an example, in the Global Go To Think Tank Index in 2015, in the category of Best Think Tank Worldwide (Non-US), the top 20 included research organisations (Chatham House and Bruegel), advocacy organisations (Transparency International and Amnesty International), government-affiliated think tanks (Danish Institute for International Studies and Stockholm International Peace Research Institute), political party-affiliated think tanks (Konrad Adenauer Foundation and Friedrich Ebert Foundation) and a cross-university network (Center for Economic Policy Research) (McGann 2016). However, many think tanks do not neatly fit into one category and instead may fall across several.

The great diversity in think tanks means that any time one makes a general statement about think tanks, it is worth asking oneself if this is accurate across the group. They differ greatly: by country, by type (independent, government, university), by aims (the target groups the think tank is trying to influence), by size (staffing and resources) and by areas of focus. It is important not to assume that think tanks are all the same.

Defining Think Tanks

The diversity among organisations that describe themselves and are described by others as "think tanks" makes it challenging to define exactly what think tanks are: it has become "a global label to identify different types of organizations" (Longhini 2015: 99). Given this, some argue that searching for an ideal definition is a futile endeavour, taking away from the important contribution these organisations are making to society and distracting from more significant questions about how to enhance and improve this contribution (Mendizabal 2010; 2014).

Nonetheless, it is important and necessary to examine the debate surrounding the definition of think tanks and to see what sets these organisations apart from other actors such as lobby groups and consulting firms. In this debate, while there is disagreement on what constitutes a think tank and what does not, all sides agree that what unites think tanks is the common objective of influencing public policymaking (Manfredi-Sanchez et al. 2015: 386; Mendizabal 2014). There is a core definition which is widely accepted which characterises think tanks as public, civil society actors which work towards improving society by bridging the academic and policy communities to tackle challenging issues facing domestic and international politics.

Where the literature is divided is between those who favour a broader definition of think tanks, with emphasis on the functions they perform, and those who insist on a narrower focus looking at organisational structure and defining think tanks by what they are not (Stone & Denham 2004: 1–2).

Minimal Definition

On the more restricted side of the spectrum, think tanks can be defined as independent, not-for-profit organisations—distinct from academia, government, the media and private sector—which seek to influence policy specifically through evidence and research-based arguments (Abelson & Lindquist 2000; Wiarda 2014).

An example of a definition of this type defines think tanks by the following essential characteristics (Gyngell 2008: 2):

- They exist for the primary purpose of undertaking applied research in public policy and shaping policy outcomes;
- They are not-for-profit institutions;
- They have a breadth of focus which can be broader or narrower, but which extends beyond a single narrow cause;
- They contribute to the public debate; that is, they conduct their principal work in the public realm.

Under such definitions, government-run, partisan and advocacy-based organisations would not be counted as genuine think tanks.

Maximal Definition

At the other end of the spectrum, under the broadest definition, a think tank can be defined as "any organisation that produces or uses research to inspire, inform or influence policy" (Mendizabal 2011). Many scholars' definitions focus less on organisational structure than on function and purpose; for example, defining think tanks as organisations that "rely on expertise" and "engage with their external environment not just in general terms, but specifically with a view to cooperating with policymakers" (Longhini 2015: 99) or as institutions devoted to analysis and research whose main goal is to influence the various actors that operate in decision-making processes (Manfredi Sanchez et al. 2015: 369).

Dr Jim McGann of the University of Pennsylvania sits on this side of the debate. According to his influential Think Tanks and Civil Society Project, think tanks are:

> public-policy research analysis and engagement organizations that generate policy-oriented research, analysis, and advice on domestic and international issues, thereby enabling policymakers and the public to make informed decisions about public policy.
>
> MCGANN 2016: 6

To put this more briefly, think tanks can be classified as organisations that undertake research, analysis and present research and advice to the public (McGann and Weaver 2000: 4). This definition encompasses think tanks that have ties with government or work on a profit-based structure. The focus for those in this camp is on the functions that these organisations perform rather than their organisational structure.

A Working Definition of Think Tanks

For the purposes of this discussion, the definition of think tanks used will be that provided by the Chinese Academy of the Social Sciences (CASS) in its *Global Think Tank Evaluation Report*. CASS is the leading academic and research centre in China with more than 31 research institutes and 45 research centres focusing on a wide variety of disciplines in the realm of philosophy, social science and public policy. While it has close links with government, as does nearly every such organisation in China, its definition of think tanks has both the virtue of simplicity and ease of application. As defined by CASS:

> a think tank is an organization exerting influence upon public policy making through independent intellectual products.
>
> CASS 2015: 3

Breaking this down, the definition includes three parts:

- An organisation (rather than an individual, such as an artist or agitator);
- Exerting influence upon public policy making (rather than as a purely academic or intellectual pursuit);
- Through independent intellectual products (which could include reports, publications, events, advice or other activities).

The CASS definition favours a broader understanding of what counts as a think tank while also incorporating elements of the narrower definition such as its focus on independent products.

This definition may not align with everyone's understanding of what a think tank is, however, it is broad enough to suit our purposes of highlighting the diversity of think tanks worldwide and exploring the various contributions they can and are making to diplomacy. In the sections that follow, this definition will be utilised to examine in what ways and how effectively think tanks contribute to diplomacy.

What is clear, however, is that there is a core definition to the concept of a think tank: that is, a group of organisations that are clearly inside a common definition of a think tank. This is set out in Figure 1. While the boundaries of the concept may be subject to debate, this does not stop the concept being useful for analysis.

The Boundary

It follows from this definition that not all organisations claiming to be think tanks are in fact deserving of that status. There may be some organisations and individuals who use the label to accrue the benefits of legitimacy afforded to think tanks without fulfilling the requirement of providing independent

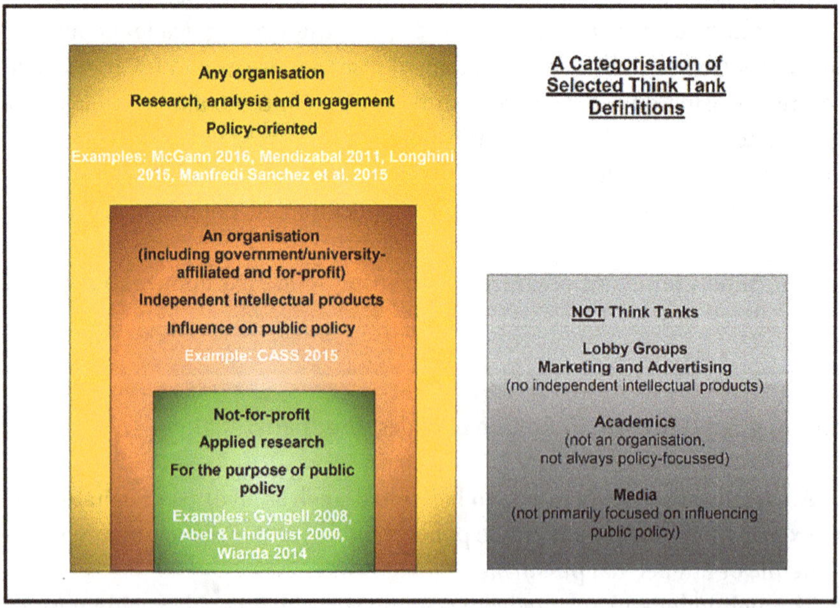

FIGURE 1 *A categorisation of selected think tank definitions*

intellectual products. For example, marketing and advertising firms are not think tanks: they are given a brief by a client of the message to be communicated and devise a creative strategy to do so. Lobbyists are in the same position, advocating a pre-defined position on behalf of others.

So, for example, the Institute of Economic Affairs in the UK and the conservative Heartland Institute in the US both describe themselves as think tanks but have a long history of being funded by tobacco and oil companies and lobbying government to argue against regulations which could jeopardise these industries (Goldenberg 2012; Monibot 2013). Such organisations do not fit the definition of think tanks if they are working solely for the pre-determined interests of their clients, producing no independent intellectual products and not considering the interests of society as a whole. We wish to make it explicit that this article is not about lobbying organisations; it does not consider these organisations as think tanks and their activities in no way fall into this discussion.

However the presence of lobbying groups in the public policy arena is undeniably muddying the reputation of think tanks and posing an issue for think tanks working to produce useful outputs for the benefit of society. There is real public concern about this more self-interested group, what Wedel (2009; 2010; 2011) variously calls a "shadow elite" or "flexians", representing a "new breed of influencers" who "flout once-sacrosanct boundaries between state and private to operate beyond the reach of government monitors and the input of publics" (2010: 27). Some lobbyists are demonstrably influential. For example, former Senator Bob Dole, now a lobbyist at law firm Alston & Bird, clearly played a role in encouraging then President-Elect Donald Trump to make an unprecedented phone call to Taiwan's President Tsai Ing-wen (Davis and Lipton 2016). The key distinction between this and the work of think tanks is that the firm was employed by the Taiwan Economic and Cultural Representative Office in the US to promote specific ends (The New York Times 2016).

To distinguish themselves from lobbyists and advocacy groups, think tanks can and are being more transparent about their funding, looking for a more diverse range of donors and projects, and being more open and accountable about their processes and methods (Drezner 2014; Drezner 2016; Wiarda 2014: 296–298; Gutbrod 2016). Individuals in think tanks will also need to be more explicit about the various roles or affiliations they may hold and make it clear in which capacity they are acting when presenting a view in the public arena.

A Note on Independence

A factor complicating the definitional debate is the issue of the independence of think tanks. Those who favour narrower definitions of think tanks insist that these organisations be completely independent organisations, for example in structure, funding and research agenda. They claim that it is the objectivity and independence of think tanks which sets them apart from other actors such as lobby groups and consulting firms, making their contribution to society of greater value (Lipton et. al. 2016; Abelson 2007: 551).

Others argue that complete independence for think tanks is unattainable (Conley Tyler 2015b). Even for those think tanks that are structurally independent, achieving complete objectivity is a challenge given that arguably, all knowledge, at least the type of knowledge in the realm of social science which is useful to policymakers, is partial, constructed and purposive (Cox 1981; Linklater 1992; Wendt 1992; Wendt 1995; Longhini 2015). The whole notion of formal think tank independence may be culturally specific. As Diane Stone (2005: 3) notes:

> [t]he notion that a think tank requires independence from the state (or corporations) in order to be 'free-thinking' is an Anglo-American norm that does not translate well into other political cultures. Increasingly, therefore, 'think tank' is conceived in terms of a policy research function and a set of analytic or policy advisory practices, rather than a specific legal organizational structure as a non-governmental, non-partisan or independent civil society entity.

This suggests a focus on whether the think tank is producing independent intellectual products rather than whether the think tank is formally an independent entity. Think tanks can reasonably have ideological outlooks (such as promoting human rights, environmental responsibility or human liberty) that inform their choice of public policy issues and the aims of their research. The crucial step is forming policy suggestions through a process of analytical rigour before these suggestions are promoted to the public and policymakers; by contrast, a lobbyist takes as given the policy suggestions of the client. CASS describes the process as follows:

> By first forming new policy suggestions based upon research and analysis, and then by publishing books, organizing various activities, and taking advantage of the mass media, etc., a think tank tries to gain the support of both the public and the relevant decision makers.
>
> CASS 2015: 2

As organisations that are seeking to influence public policy, think tanks are often required to be advocates for specific positions and look for strategic avenues to improve their visibility and funding (Wiarda 2014: 272; Krishna 2014). For this reason, they may take on a role which could entail a very close relationship with policymakers or any other defined target audience (Longhini 2015: 103).

Understandably, this blurring of boundaries has led to confusion, even consternation, by some observers who see think tanks' mimicry of the tactics of lobbyists and advocacy groups as jeopardising their reputation as independent, non-partisan institutions (Lipton & Williams 2016; Lipton et al. 2016). This criticism has been particularly levelled towards think tanks in the US where some organisations are viewed as increasingly governed by corporate interests with limited disclosure of this cooperation.

Arguably what this points to is more an issue of transparency than independence. As Drezner (2014) notes, the fact that we live in a "world of special interests" is unavoidable. Initiatives like Transparify encourage think tanks to make the funding of their research public to deal with the perception that funding may have bought influence over think tanks' results (Gutbrod 2016).

The definition used in this paper focuses on the independence of think tanks' intellectual products rather than their formal independence as institutions. Case studies cover a diverse group of organisations exerting influence upon public policymaking through independent intellectual products: including government-funded and for-profit groups; organisations located within government and on university campus; and, of course the not-for-profit organisations that fall within the core definition of think tanks.

Discussion focuses less on independence of structure than on independence of function, described by Mendizabal 2014 as including:

- Providing ideas (including popularising ideas), people, access to power;
- Creating, maintaining, opening spaces for debate;
- As boundary workers or windows into the policymaking process—and into other spaces;
- Channels of intellectual resources to political parties, interest groups, leaders;
- Legitimising ideas, policies and practices—and individuals or groups;
- Monitoring and auditing public policy and behaviour;
- Public and elite (including policymakers) education.

Think tanks might best be judged by the contribution they are making to bring various communities together and to improve society and the nature of the public debate rather than by how independent or objective they are (Conley Tyler 2015b).

Think Tanks as Knowledge-Brokers

A useful way to conceptualise think tanks is as liminal: that is, occupying a space on the boundaries of various communities. As Mendizabal (2016) notes, think tanks are boundary workers due to their ability to:

- Appreciate and undertake research (boundary with academia);
- Communicate effectively to broader audiences and the public (boundary with the media);
- Undertake analysis and deliver solutions (boundary with consultancy);
- Analyse policy and provide actionable recommendations (boundary with policy and politics);
- Work with citizens to develop new ideas and solutions (boundary with NGOs).

In part think tanks do this by using different forms of language adapted to their main audiences: the languages of public policy; of the media; of academia; and of the digital world (Manfredi 2014). Arguably this is greatly needed in the case of academia and policy where there exists a significant divide.

The Academic-Policy Divide

In many areas of policy there exists a worrying gap between the academic and policymaking worlds. Both have developed into distinct communities which are governed by different cultures and understandings of what counts as valuable knowledge (Conley Tyler 2015c).

In the academic world, the focus is on developing theoretical rigour, scientific methodology, scholarly objectivity and a long-term perspective on phenomena. Knowledge of the world 'out there' is pursued for its own sake, with success measured by how one's research is accepted by one's peers and the academic community (Bailes et al. 2011: 23). This leads to a culture where the pinnacle of academic achievement is a new conceptual theory and a "tendency toward ever narrower and more arcane study" (Lowenthal and Bertucci 2014). Some academics fear too close a relationship with those in power and even those that aspire to have an impact on policy often have an unrealistic idea of policy-relevance (Byman and Kroenig 2016: 292).

Policymakers act under vastly different constraints and incentives. For policymakers, useful knowledge is that which is practical, detailed, specific and aids in improving the social world (Gould-Davies 2010: 4). They do not have the luxury of time to deliberate issues but are required to act fast and take decisions with often limited information. Among policy circles, the adjective 'academic' can be used as a synonym for 'irrelevant'. Many people involved in the development of public policies see academic researchers as failing to take the reality of policy into account in setting research questions (Shergold 2005). They also find the focus on complex theories and jargon-ridden research unhelpful (Avey and Desch 2014: 228).

Despite this gap, there are certain inputs that each community can use and wants from the other. While many policymakers ignore academic research as irrelevant, many find the considered insights and the contextual background provided by academics into an issue highly useful (Del Rosso 2015: 128). According to Avey and Desch (2014: 243), "the thing policymakers most want from scholars are frameworks for making sense of the world they have to operate in."

More needs to be done to ensure that academic research has an influence on policy, for example by ensuring that research is timely, disseminated at the right time and in the right format and is promoted through linkages and visibility (Byman & Kroenig 2016: 291). These are some areas where think tanks can prove particularly useful.

How Think Tanks Bridge the Divide

Think tanks can be seen as a form of "knowledge-broker", a concept that has gained prominence in recent years to describe those working to mend the gap between social science research and the development of public policy (CHSRF 2003), but which can be used more generally for any organisation that attempts to transfer knowledge (Conley Tyler, Matthews and Dietrich 2017).

In terms of function, knowledge brokers generally facilitate the transfer of knowledge from where it is abundant to where it is needed, thereby improving innovative capacity. As Steen (2010) puts it: "Knowledge brokers aren't insiders; they are on the edge of two or more communities. It's a precarious position to be in and knowledge brokers need to work hard to stay involved with multiple groups with different cultures and expertise".

Think tanks can play an important role as knowledge brokers: occupying a place between government and academia, they act as ideal links between the research and policymaking worlds. Given their liminal position, they are able to operate in both worlds while simultaneously maintaining their distance. As Medvetz (2008: 6) puts it, this often involves "a complex performance made of equal parts distancing and affinity." As bridge institutions, the role of think tanks is to convert knowledge into practice, to act as a 'transmission belt' for ideas to policymakers (Conley Tyler 2015b).

McGann & Weaver (2000) identify five key roles that think tanks play: as a mediator between government and the public; as an investigator identifying and evaluating key issues or proposals; as a transformer of ideas and problems into policy; as an informed voice within debate; and as a forum provider for the exchange of views, ideas and information. Many of these are knowledge-broker roles.

A core function central to most think tanks is transforming analysis into understandable language and advice for the target community. They can reframe and filter academic research to present it in a way that is understandable and appealing to policymakers (Wiarda 2014: 276; Longhini 2015: 100). In addition, given their valuable connections with policymakers, think tanks can serve as facilitators of issues and the exchange of ideas. Through interactions with policy advisors, whether it be orally, in written communications or as hosts to a seminar, think tanks serve as interpreters and evaluators (McGann & Weaver 2000: 6). They also provide a platform to share ideas, bringing together experts and combatants in a forum for discussion. They can frame issues in a new way, informing the uninformed and helping to shape the debate, and play a central role in facilitating the connectivity of ideas (Conley Tyler 2015a; Manfredi-Sanchez et al. 2015: 368).

As Gyngell (2008: 5) summarises it, think tanks perform a role in structuring the public debate on key issues of interest to the government, policy advisors, the public and others, helping to "shape the way we think about the world by providing an alternative source of well-considered views about how we should understand the world". They improve the quality of debate by working to 'anchor' the debate in research-based evidence which, unlike scholarly institutions, "is shaped more heavily by the parameters of public policy" (Gyngell 2008: 5). They produce new ideas by responding quickly to emerging issues and developments. Think tanks can also 'float' ideas that are too risky for governments; they can more easily bring together groups with different interests to work through problems and they can facilitate 'second track diplomacy' (Gyngell 2008: 5). Thus, they can use their role as experts to facilitate policy-relevant research and more evidence-based, inclusive policymaking (Ambrus et al. 2014: 5–6).

Think tanks undertake a variety of knowledge-broker roles including: agenda-setting, research, evidence-gathering, analysis, dialogue, knowledge transfer and dissemination of ideas to the public. Specific products include the hosting of events, briefings and seminars; publication of books, issue briefs, blog posts, opinion pieces and newspaper commentary; and the provision of oral or written advice (McGann & Weaver 2000: 5). Think tanks have the necessary expertise, contacts, resources, reputation and tactics to make them useful intermediaries and influential actors in the diplomatic landscape (Wiarda 2014: 272, 299). It is their unique position and their role as knowledge brokers that distinguishes think tanks from other civil society organisations, public and private institutions working to influence public policy.

Measuring Think Tank Effectiveness

While think tanks perform a range of different roles in their attempt to influence public policy, not all think tanks perform these functions well, either due to contextual constraints or because of poor organisational management. As public policy-focused institutions, it is important that their activities are scrutinised and held to account based on a set of common indicators. However, the task of measuring think tank effectiveness is nearly as difficult as attempting to reach a consensus on what think tanks are. That being said, various attempts to measure think tank effectiveness have been made and are outlined below.

The leading index of think tanks, the University of Pennsylvania's Global Go to Think Tanks Index, is primarily a reputation index: it ranks the world's leading think tanks through voting by 6,846 think tanks and more than 4,750 journalists, policymakers, public and private donors, and functional and regional area specialists worldwide (McGann 2017). Respondents are asked to take into account a list of 28 nomination and ranking criteria (20–22); however, in reality survey respondents can rank according to any criteria they wish. The index is not designed to track output or impact, in the way that a funder might require for project evaluation. The core goal of the index is to increase the profile of think tanks and raise public awareness of the important role think tanks play in government and civil societies around the globe.

As someone who thinks deeply about how to measure think tank performance, Dr Jim McGann has suggested some useful indicators to take into account when contemplating the impact of think tanks (McGann 2017: 23):

- "*Resource indicators*: Ability to recruit and retain leading scholars and analysts; the level, quality, and stability of financial support; proximity and access to decision-makers and other policy elites; and key contacts in the policy academic communities, and the media."
- "*Utilization indicators*: Reputation as a "go-to" organization by media and policy elites in the country; quantity and quality of media appearances and citations, web hits, testimony before legislative and executive bodies; briefings, official appointments, consultation by officials or departments/ agencies; books sold; reports distributed; references made to research and analysis in scholarly and popular publications and attendees at conferences and seminars organized."

- "*Output indicators*: Number and quality of: policy proposals and ideas generated; publications produced (books, journal articles, policy briefs, etc.); briefings, conferences, and seminars organized."
- "*Impact indicators*: Recommendations considered or adopted by policymakers and civil society organizations; issue network centrality; awards granted; publication in or citation of publications in academic journals, public testimony and the media that influences the policy debate and decision-making."

Most think tanks would collect and report information on the each of these to some extent. The easiest are output, resource and utilisation indicators; the hardest are impact indicators where it is difficult to judge issues like influence on policy and decision-making. Assessing the impact of think tanks is no easy endeavour to undertake given the various and conflicting actors, events, and politics involved in the policymaking process.

The Chinese Academy of Social Sciences' *Global Think Tanks Evaluation Report 2015* evaluates think tanks according to three main levels: attractive power, management power and impact power (CASS 2015: 22). According to this model, attractive power refers to the external environment of the think tank, meaning that the more favourable a think tank's external environment is the more likely it is to attract more resources and enhance attraction. It also refers to the think tank's external reputation, attractiveness to staff and outcome attractiveness. As to 'management power,' this factor refers to the ability of think tank managers to manage and develop the think tank, including strategy, structure, system, staff style and shared values. The third factor, 'impact power' refers to the expression of a think tank and the embodiment of the attractive and management powers. It incorporates a consideration of the think tank's influence on policy, academia and society and its international influence.

In 2015, CASS evaluated a selected group of think tanks utilising these three levels of attractive power, management power and impact power. It is yet to be seen if this is a model that will be broadly adopted.

One other attempt to rank think tanks focuses on encouraging them to report on the funding of their activities. Transparify rates the extent to which think tanks publicly disclose through their websites the source of their funding in order to enable 'citizens, journalists, researchers and policy makers to distinguish, at a glance, the transparent from the opaque.' It argues that transparency can bring "huge benefits in terms of signalling to the public its commitment to intellectual independence, integrity, excellence in research, and the credibility that comes from respecting democratic norms while participating in democratic debates" (Gutbrod 2016: 2). Institutions rated with five stars are considered highly transparent on the source of their funds while those ranked with four stars are considered broadly transparent, such as where they group donors by categories (Gutbrod, 2016: 3). On the other end of the spectrum, think tanks awarded zero or one star are considered 'highly opaque' for choosing not to disclose the identity and source of funds donated (Gutbrod, 2016: 3).

The current situation is that there is no commonly agreed metric for measuring think tanks' effectiveness. While the success of a think tank may be best judged through consideration of the quality of the think tank's work, its independence and impact on policy (Conley Tyler 2015b), there is not yet an easy way to demonstrate effectiveness.

Given the diversity in the think tank landscape today, reaching a common metric to evaluate their effectiveness will be a difficult task. Nonetheless, it is important for each think tank to have some system of self-evaluation to examine ways in which it can innovate and enhance its contribution to society.

This work, however, will not attempt to measure the effectiveness of specific think tanks. Instead, in the chapters that follow, it will aim to illustrate ways in which think tanks contribute to diplomacy.

Part 2. Understanding Modern Diplomacy

There was a time when it would have seemed absurd to even suggest that non-officials might have any role in diplomacy. But the nature of diplomacy has changed greatly with increased recognition of the role of non-state actors.

Non-State Actors in International Relations and Diplomacy

Non-state actors have long been recognised as playing a role in international affairs. For example, theorist of international society Hedley Bull recognised that the term diplomacy must be applied to the "official relation not only of states but also of other political entities with standing in world politics" (1977: 157):

> Great uncertainty still surrounds the application to diplomatic relationships, involving entities other than the sovereign state, of rules and procedures evolved in interstate diplomacy … Yet it is clear that entities other than states have standing as actors in world politics, and that they are engaged in diplomacy vis-à-vis states and one another.

In recent years, non-state actors have grown in number and influence (Thakur 2013). The non-state actor encompasses a range of entities who have established themselves in international relations as influential figures including:

> supranational and intergovernmental organisations, NGOs, uncivil society organisations like terrorist groups, arms and drug smugglers, and human traffickers, multinational corporations, philanthropic foundations, celebrities, transnational professional associations which establish global standards and norms and constitute networked global governance and individuals.
>
> THAKUR 2013: 73

As the visibility of non-state actors in international relations has increased, the literature on non-state actors has grown, taking up the task of considering the role, nature and influence of non-state actors in international relations (Neumann 2011; Keck & Sikkink 1999; Cooper & Hocking 2000; Forma & Seggar 2006; Kelley 2010). New strands of thought can now be located within the literature on diplomacy, which now includes the study of traditional diplomacy, the role of non-state actors and the emergence of non-state actors as diplomatic actors. Indeed, the growth of non-state actors in the diplomatic landscape invites an exploration of the role of non-state actors in international relations, their relationship with governments, and the nature of their status within the traditional Westphalian system. On the changing nature of international diplomacy, Neumann (2011: 528) has noted that "non-governmental organisations have become more visible in world politics through delegation and indirect rule, thereby opening a new state-society interfaces at the global level."

While traditionally state and civil society actors have been defined in opposition to each other, the complexity of the international environment today has led both to see the value in collaborating with the other to address common problems. Thus, states have drawn on civil society actors such as non-government organisations (NGOs) to extend their own diplomatic reach, while NGOs have used the power of the state to pursue their own agendas (Cooper & Hocking 2000: 367, Hocking 2004: 149). Civil society actors can function as intermediaries of the state at the local level in a foreign society. They offer states tailored expertise and policy advice, and carry out diplomatic functions where official state diplomats may find it difficult to reach (Sending et al. 2011: 528, Hocking 2013: 132, Kelley 2010: 289).

Non-state actors such as NGOs and think tanks possess particular strengths as diplomatic actors which states have recognised and harnessed in conducting their own diplomatic activity. Their authority lies in working for the benefit of humankind which gives these actors transnational support and greater credibility with the international public. The advocacy that NGOs undertake in the name of human rights or the environment, for example, appeals to a transnational constituency. This gives non-state actors a wide reach and a strong pool of resources to draw from in order to launch their activities. They are central actors in what Keck and Sikkink (1999) call 'transnational advocacy networks' whereby they create links between government, business and civil society, set the terms of the debate on certain issues, bring new ideas and norms into policy discussions, provide alternative sources of information and, in this way, exercise growing power and influence in world affairs. Additionally, non-state actors have also proven adept at deploying new technology and social media to strengthen their cause and garner funding. This broad-based support is something that national governments may be lacking which makes them eager to include non-state actors such as think tanks in decision-making forums for greater credibility.

In this context, as non-state actors with growing power and influence in international affairs, it appears more conceivable that think tanks might be involved in diplomacy.

The Evolution of Diplomacy

Diplomacy is a centuries-old social practice with its own ceremonial and procedural culture that has been passed down through different diplomatic generations. Diplomatic practice is tied to the birth of the nation-state whereby countries exchanged emissaries and ambassadors in order to manage their developing relations with each other. The functions and privileges of these agents were codified in international law with the *Vienna Convention on Diplomatic Relations 1961*.

To some observers, this continuity in diplomatic tradition and the strict observance of diplomatic formalities is evidence of the stagnation of diplomacy (Ross 2015: 4). While there is some truth in claims that diplomacy has failed to keep pace with the remarkable progress the world has undergone, bringing into question its relevance as an institution in international relations (Wiseman 1999: 43; Heine 2008: 273–274), it is also true that there are numerous and nuanced ways in which diplomacy has evolved.

Diplomatic scholars have characterised the evolution of diplomacy in various ways including 'old' and 'new' diplomacy, 'club' versus 'networked diplomacy', and traditional versus 'integrative', 'polylateral', 'catalytic' and 'mega' diplomacy (Heine 2008; Hocking et al. 2012; Wiseman 1999; Wiseman 2000; Hocking 1999; Khanna 2011). The 'old' or 'club' model of diplomacy was hierarchical and elitist in nature as it involved a small number of official state diplomats who interacted with their counterparts in other states, carried out their functions largely in secret and confined themselves to the bureaucratic processes of the state (Heine 2008: 273).

Due to changes in the international arena in the 20th century, the nature of diplomatic activity has changed significantly. An important driver of diplomatic change in recent history was World War I where the failure of old forms of secretive, elitist diplomacy were seen as a primary factor leading to the outbreak of the war and a new type of diplomacy was called for (Wilson quoted in Jönsson & Hall 2005: 12).

Diplomacy today has become much more multilateral or polylateral in character, even though bilateral diplomacy between official representatives of states is still a crucial part of modern diplomacy. Developments in transportation and communication technologies, the rise of non-state actors and the emergence of new security challenges have created pressures on the institution of diplomacy to develop (Wiseman 1999: 40–41). Seen from one point of view, "Diplomats today are essentially tasked with helping their own countries navigate the perils of globalisation" (Heine 2013: 278).

To aid in this task, foreign ministries and their diplomatic agents are increasingly incorporating new actors into the traditional realm of diplomacy. This has been labelled polylateral, integrative or catalytic diplomacy involving greater collaboration between traditional state diplomats and new diplomatic actors who in many ways are taking over and expanding the tasks of traditional diplomacy (Hocking 1999: 31, 34, Malone 2013: 137; Wiseman 1999; Wiseman 2000). For example, second track or Track II diplomacy, a term first coined by US State Department official Joseph Montville (1991) refers to diplomatic interaction between individuals who are not agents of the state. It can be beneficial especially in the realm of conflict resolution, however, has also been employed in the conduct of economic and security relations, particularly when official negotiations are stalled or non-existent; it provides a backdoor channel of communication.

These trends mean that diplomacy is no longer the sole preserve of the state but now involves the participation of various non-state actors who have a greater degree of flexibility in launching diplomatic initiatives (Arbour 2009; Kraft 2000: 350; Langhorne 2005: 331). It can be argued that these new diplomatic actors are performing the functions of traditional diplomacy in both the activities that they undertake and methods that they utilise. It is clear that diplomacy today is much more than what official, state diplomats do. As Gregory posits, "Diplomacy increasingly takes place in layers above, below, and beyond the state" (2014: 5).

Networked diplomacy is much more transparent and fast-paced, involving both official state diplomats and a plethora of new actors. However, networked diplomacy has not led to a complete abandonment of the past. Instead, it has led to the "reinventing of old methods and practices in new circumstances" so that diplomacy today is characterised by the interplay of the old with the new (Weisbrode 2014). Diplomacy is no longer tied to the institution of the sovereign state but exists across and beyond the state system. More than simply strengthening the ties between states, diplomacy is now about strengthening the links between diverse polities and cultures. For this reason, diplomacy has become a much more participatory activity. Or, in other words, "Increasingly, there is more diplomacy in civil society and more civil society in diplomacy" (Gregory 2015: 10).

If diplomacy can be defined variously by *who* is acting, the *activity* being undertaken and the *manner* in which it is undertaken (Wiseman & Sharp 2017), it is suggested that it is more appropriate now to define diplomacy by the activity/diplomatic function and by diplomatic culture rather than by actor.

Viewing diplomacy as a social practice or behaviour better portrays the plurality which characterises the diplomacy of the 21st century (Jönsson & Hall 2005: 21, Kelley 2010: 286). Geoffrey Wiseman argues convincingly that there is a distinctive diplomatic culture—made up of accumulated norms, rules and institutions—which are widely accepted and internalised by those in international society (Wiseman 2005), even if there are variations in style and substance among individual countries' diplomats (Wiseman 2011).

Understanding Diplomatic Functions

If diplomacy is understood as a set of behaviours, rather than something intrinsic to specific individuals, it is possible to characterise various diplomatic functions.

The classic definition provided by the *Vienna Convention on Diplomatic Relations 1961* is a useful starting point. In Article 3 it describes the function of a diplomatic mission as follows:

a) representing the sending state in the receiving state;
b) protecting the interests of the sending state and of its nationals;
c) negotiating with the government of the receiving state;
d) ascertaining and reporting on conditions and developments in the receiving state;
e) promoting friendly relations between the sending state and the receiving state, and developing their economic, cultural and scientific relations.

Of these, only one is definitionally impossible for think tanks to fulfil: the function of representation given that they are not official agents of the state. The remainder could potentially be performed by think tanks. While the second function of 'protecting interests' could be read in a narrow sense of a consular function, it can also be viewed in a broader sense as "promoting the national interest (which encompasses political, economic, cultural and social interests)" in the words of the French Ministry of Foreign Affairs and International Development (2017).

As the understanding of diplomacy has developed to incorporate communication with entities other than states, so the understanding of diplomatic functions has changed. For example, two decades following the Vienna Convention, noted theorist Hedley Bull (1982) identified five key functions of diplomacy:

- communication;
- negotiation of agreements;
- gathering of intelligence or information;
- minimisation of friction between states in international relations;
- symbolising the 'existence of the society of states'.

He defined the function of communication as between "the political leaders of states and other entities in world politics", recognising that communications can extend beyond the traditional state-to-state.

Moving to the current day, communications outside government-to-government channels have become a key part of diplomacy, whether conceptualised as "public diplomacy" or as the "public dimension that is now central in diplomatic practice" (Gregory 2015). Geoffrey Wiseman outlines how states have added to their bilateral and multilateral interaction with other states a third dimension—'polylateralism'—where they interact with non-state actors (Wiseman 2000).

Any modern definition of diplomatic functions needs to include these aspects. Recent outlines of the core diplomatic functions tend to include communication in the broad sense, such as Rebecca Adler-Nissen (2016) who identifies three main roles for diplomats: communication, negotiation and advocacy.

The Potential Role of Think Tanks in Diplomacy

Using the definitions above, this paper will focus on four diplomatic functions that can potentially be undertaken by think tanks:

- negotiation between states;
- communication with foreign publics;

- information-gathering and reporting;
- promoting friendly relations and minimising friction in international affairs.[8]

This is a non-exclusive list and we leave open what other diplomatic functions might be identified or evolve over time.

For the purposes of this article, it is sufficient if think tanks through their various activities can be shown to be contributing to these functions, either directly or indirectly, within the norms of diplomatic culture. If so, they are playing a role in diplomacy by fulfilling functions and roles that traditionally rested with diplomatic actors.

While it is important not to fall into the trap of defining every cross-border interaction as "diplomacy", there are examples where non-officials perform functions that can reasonably be described as diplomatic and, importantly, "governments and other stakeholders regard them as legitimate governance actors" in doing so (Gregory 2015:13).

Before we go on, it is important to note that even when think tanks fulfil diplomatic functions, that does not transform them into diplomats as the term is generally understood. Public international law remains crucial to the practice of diplomacy and plays a vital role in guiding how diplomats work with each other and how diplomats are to be treated. International rules and norms on the practice of diplomacy remains the 'backbone' of all diplomatic activities and procedures from Hugo Grotius' rights of ambassadors stated in the in the seventeenth century (Grotius 2012: 261) to the codification of formal rules in the Vienna Convention in 1961 which make mission premises inviolable, extend protection to diplomats working within the embassy, afford immunity to diplomats from criminal jurisdiction and oblige the host state to protect communication lines between embassy and the sending state. None of these protections apply to think tanks, whatever role they might be playing.

Putting the suggested four functions of diplomacy together with either a direct or an indirect contribution generates a matrix of the potential involvement of think tanks in diplomacy which identifies eight potential contributions of think tanks as follows:

8 Hedley Bull (1982) identifies friction between states in international relations as unavoidable: given the 'juxtaposition of different communities, each with its own values, preoccupations, prejudices and sensibilities, friction in international relations is always present'. It is the task of diplomacy to manage, contain and ease the effects of friction.

TABLE 1 *Functions of think tanks in diplomacy*

	Negotiation	Communication	Information-gathering	Friendly Relations
Direct	Hired Guns	Charm Offensive	Témoignage	Safe Space
Indirect	School for Diplomats	Personal Trainers	Chief Knowledge Officer	Wise Council

Negotiation

Direct

Where a think tank directly contributes to diplomatic negotiations by providing inputs as advisors before and during negotiations.

Indirect

Where a think tank provides training or support to diplomats to assist them in conducting negotiations, for example, through training courses or negotiation workshops.

Communication

Direct

Where a think tank directly communicates with and aims to influence foreign publics whether through its website, its publications or the participation of its researchers in events and debate.

Indirect

Where a think tank assists officials in improving their communication with foreign publics. This could take the form of providing a training manual on how to conduct public diplomacy or formal training and coaching.

Information-Gathering and Reporting

Direct

Where a think tank gathers information and reports it, including acting as a witness ("temoignage"). This can be it through fact-finding, a formal report and online media.

Indirect

Where a think tank assists government in its information-gathering, for example through agenda-setting or providing advice to government in improving its information-gathering.

Promoting Friendly Relations and Minimising Friction

Direct

Where a think tank provides a forum for officials to engage with each other and discuss issues openly, for example, through a conference or annual gathering of leaders.

Indirect

Where a think tank provides advice to states on how they can improve their relations. This could include policy briefs, reports or hosting forums or meetings which include key decision-makers.

Each of the elements of this matrix is considered in detail in the case studies that follow. While this outline of diplomatic functions is not exhaustive—diplomatic functions could be identified and classified in a range of ways in more or fewer categories—if these are accepted as at least some of the functions of diplomacy, it provides a standard against which the work of think tanks can be judged. If think tanks can be shown to be fulfilling these functions, it demonstrates that think tanks are contributing both directly and indirectly to the conduct of diplomacy.

Judging the Significance of Think Tanks' Contribution

The diversity in the think tank landscape can make it difficult to judge how significant think tanks' contribution to diplomacy might be and this is not something we aspire to do in this work.

As discussed in Chapter 1, the term "think tank" can describe organisations of different shapes and sizes with widely varying degrees of financial strength, levels of independence, influence and types of work performed (Stone 2000: 2). Reasonable expectations of one organisation might be entirely unrealistic for another.

Additionally, the only people in a reasonable position to judge are hardly disinterested observers: officials will be reluctant to admit that they were influenced or assisted by any non-official actors, as this diminishes their agency and prestige; similarly, think tanks have incentives beyond mere self-regard to rate their contributions as highly influential, given that this will assist in attracting future funding. Even when a think tank believes it can 'see its fingerprints' on the result, it is sometimes inadvisable for a think tank to claim credit (Conley Tyler 2015b).

Even if a disinterested observer were able to give an objective assessment, it would still be difficult to tease out which outcomes came from which inputs. A diplomatic outcome like "an improved image for country X among the citizens of country Y" has many antecedents: some official, some non-official; some immediate, some longer term. It is nigh on impossible accurately to assign responsibility for a specific outcome to a single diplomatic input.

Thus, the case studies that follow are not designed to judge and compare think tanks. Rather, through them we hope to illustrate in practice how various think tanks are contributing to diplomacy today.

Part 3. Case Studies of Think Tanks in Diplomacy

Below, eight case studies are provided to illustrate the direct and indirect contribution of think tanks to four diplomatic functions: negotiation, communication, information-gathering and promoting friendly relations and minimisation of friction in international relations. Out of a number of possible examples, case studies have been selected from different regions as set out below. A concluding case study shows how a single organisation attempts to work across the various diplomatic functions.

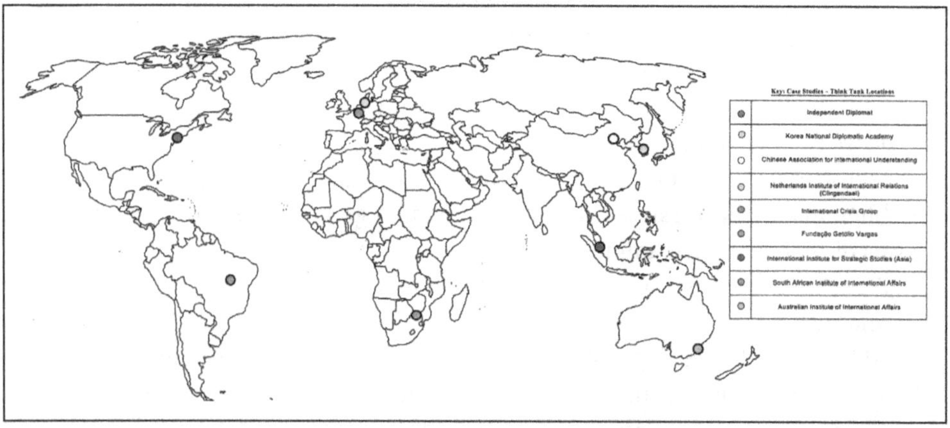

FIGURE 2 *Case studies—think tank locations*

1 *Direct Negotiation: Think Tanks as "Hired Guns"*

Negotiation is a subtle art and is one of the perennial skills required of diplomatic actors. According to Hedley Bull (2002: 173), the "diplomatic profession … is a repository of specialist skills and techniques in the business of negotiation." The role of diplomats is to facilitate the achievement of common interest through their knowledge of the parties involved as well as their skills of persuasion and communication (Bull 2002: 174):

> [The diplomat] seeks always to reason or persuade rather than to bully or threaten. He tries to show that the objective for which he is seeking is consistent with the other party's interests, as well as with his own. He prefers to speak of 'rights' rather than of 'demands', and to show that these rights flow from rules or principles which both states hold in common, and which the other state has already conceded.

While diplomats are not the only conduit for negotiation between governments—for example government departments may negotiate directly with their counterparts in other countries—negotiation remains a core diplomatic skill. For the least wealthy states and newly-emerged or emerging states, lack of resources, experience and know-how are significant hurdles to overcome. This is an area where think tanks can potentially assist.

Independent Diplomat

Independent Diplomat is a non-profit organisation that provides what could broadly be described as diplomatic services to states, emerging states and other actors in need of its assistance. This case study examines its mandate and activities, looking in particular at its role carrying out the diplomatic function of negotiation on behalf of its clients. While there are many examples of individual former politicians and diplomats fulfilling diplomatic functions, in what Andrew Cooper has characterised as "diplomatic afterlives" (2015), the founder of Independent Diplomat, British diplomat Carne Ross, is unusual in having established an organisation rather than simply providing his own services.

Independent Diplomat does not bill itself as a think tank—it describes itself as a "unique, non-profit advisory group in the world of diplomacy" (2017)—but it would fit within some of the wider definitions of a think tank as an organisation that produces independent intellectual outputs to exert an influence on policy. While it works for specific clients, Independent Diplomat does not consider itself involved in lobbying or advocacy: it views itself as a consultancy, "giving expert advice on all aspects of the practice of diplomacy".[9] This case study illustrates its work, some of its successes and the challenges it encounters in carrying out its functions.

About Independent Diplomat: History, Mission and Activities

Independent Diplomat was founded in 2004 by former British diplomat Carne Ross as the "world's first diplomatic advisory firm" (Ross quoted in Gray 2013) comprised of former diplomats and other experts to provide diplomatic representation and strategic advice to clients. Ross was motivated by the realisation that those most affected by diplomatic decisions were often not included in discussions about their fate. He noticed an apparent imbalance between the most and least wealthy states in their access to resources to participate in diplomacy:

> I wanted to try to remedy the diplomatic deficit I had witnessed at the Security Council. The idea was to establish a network of experienced practitioners (former diplomats, international lawyers and skilled analysts) whose expertise would be available to help small, inexperienced or under-resources countries and political groups with their diplomacy—a diplomatic service for those who need it most.
>
> ROSS 2007: 192

Independent Diplomat "works inside the diplomatic system to ensure that the voices of the people most affected by international decisions are heard in the negotiations about their futures" (2016). It offers a range of services with a core aim to "improve the diplomatic performance of its clients across the three pillars of diplomacy": political strategy; international law; and public diplomacy and media (Independent Diplomat 2017).

The organisation is small in size but transnational, with 25 staff based in offices in London, New York, Hargeisa and Somaliland. They specialise in providing expert impartial advice, strategic direction and diplomatic representation on wide-ranging topics including, but not limited to, the United Nations and its various organs, the European Union, climate change, natural resources, human rights, public international law, international humanitarian law, law of the sea and issues relating to foreign direct investment. Ross explains that this

9 Email correspondence with Alana Esposito, Public Relations Coordinator at Independent Diplomat, 5 January 2017.

can include "communications to the UN Security Council, speeches or formal diplomatic presentations" (Ross 2007: 192).

As a non-government, non-profit organisation, Independent Diplomat relies upon donations and fees from financially able clients to fund its work. In selecting its clients, Independent Diplomat has a "strict criteria", selecting only those "committed to democracy and the protection of human rights" (Ross quoted in Gray 2013). To ensure observance of this rule, it undertakes due diligence to ensure a potential client meets its standards. While all clients pay a fee for services provided, this is calculated in accordance with the state's "ability to pay and the demands of the project" (Independent Diplomat 2017). As Ross emphasises, Independent Diplomat is "very much at the service of [its] clients" (Ross quoted in Ladek 2015).

Independent Diplomat and Negotiation

A key part of Independent Diplomat's work is to provide services to clients to improve their diplomatic negotiation and representation. It aims to assist its clients understand diplomatic processes, navigate the complex territory of international diplomacy and advocate their interests (Independent Diplomat 2017). Services include both providing strategic advice to clients which they then implement in their international interactions and, at a more direct level, for Independent Diplomat staff to provide diplomatic representation, preparation of diplomatic communication and speeches, building diplomatic relations and coordination of diplomatic visits.

Between 2004 and 2007, Independent Diplomat represented its first client, the government of the newly-emerging state of Kosovo. When Ross went to Kosovo as United Nations Coordinator it dawned on him that being excluded from discussions about their status was one factor motivating the Kosovar's turn to violence. He realised that the people of Kosovo "needed a diplomat to advocate for their interests", a role which Ross took on by offering his services to the leaders of the Kosovar people (Kohlenberg 2015). He ensured they were included at the diplomatic table at the United Nations in New York where their fate was being decided. In that period, Independent Diplomat gathered information, relayed advice and assisted the government of Kosovo to understand the UN negotiation processes and helped it articulate its interests to the powerful decision-makers in New York. Since then, Independent Diplomat has made it its business to advise struggling governments and peoples in their preparation for international negotiations and has, at times, acted on behalf of some clients as their representative in these negotiations.

Independent Diplomat was instrumental in aiding the people of South Sudan to gain independence in 2011. Through Ross's understanding of the UN system and processes, he succeeded in assisting a delegation from South Sudan into the viewing gallery at the UN where the Security Council was deliberating South Sudan's referendum for independence. Despite being a serious breach of convention, Ross's efforts led to South Sudanese leaders getting a seat at the table where they articulated South Sudan's aspirations for peace and independence (Odone 2012). The relationship did not end there, with Independent Diplomat experts going on to work closely with the leadership of South Sudan from 2004–2009 in Juba as well as in its foreign embassies and missions to improve South Sudan's diplomatic representation and to provide strategic advice and coordination.

Recently, Independent Diplomat has also assisted the Syrian National Coalition and the High Negotiations Committee which represents the political opposition at the UN-sponsored Geneva II and Geneva III peace talks. It has helped enhance the opposition's influence in key diplomatic centres, facilitating visits between representatives of the opposition and civil society with officials and decision-makers worldwide (2017). As a result of its support, the Syrians have been able to impose more effective sanctions again the Syrian government, highlighted widespread atrocities by the regime, put forward effective policy ideas in international fora and developed mechanisms to better ensure civilian safety.

In February 2017, Independent Diplomat listed its current projects on its website as follows:

- Paving the Way for a Peaceful, Democratic Syria (the Syrian National Coalition);
- Justice in Sri Lanka (US Tamil Political Action Council);
- Tackling Climate Change (Republic of the Marshall Islands and the High Ambition Coalition);
- Western Sahara (Government of the Saharawi Arab Democratic Republic);
- Somaliland (Republic of Somaliland).

Successes

Independent Diplomat has established itself as a unique diplomatic advisory group providing advice and representation in diplomatic processes on behalf of the least wealthy states. It has demonstrated its commitment to representing its clients as part of negotiations, providing political strategy advice and promoting understanding of diplomatic processes.

It can boast a number of successes. It has played a key role in the Geneva II peace talks on the current situation in Syria, successfully represented the Republic of the Marshall Islands as part of negotiations under the UNFCCC and advised Kosovo, Croatia, Moldova, the government of the Republic of South Sudan and Cyprus on diplomatic strategy, communication and negotiations.

Since 2009 Independent Diplomat has acted on behalf of the Republic of the Marshall Islands as part of negotiations under the UN Framework Convention on Climate Change (UNFCCC). It is credited with playing a key role in negotiations and for providing an effective voice to the Marshall Islands, including increasing its role in the Cartagena Dialogue for Progressive Action and hosting the 2013 Pacific Islands Leaders' Meeting.

More recently, Independent Diplomat helped the Marshall Islands emerge as a leader on climate change action. The country played an instrumental role in the success of the 2015 Paris Agreement on Climate Change, gathering a coalition of over 100 countries—the High Ambition Coalition—which pushed for the agreement to be more robust and strict, showing that "even very small countries can have an outsized influence in diplomatic processes that involve bigger countries" (Ross quoted in Cassauwers 2016).

Specifically, Independent Diplomat contributed to these negotiations by preparing Marshallese officials for high-level international climate negotiations and diplomatic meetings. As a result, it has now become an expert organisation in the area of international climate change policy and its negotiation work in this area has "helped the organisation establish itself as a diplomatic force alongside its clients" (Independent Diplomat 2016).

Independent Diplomat had impeccable timing: as a niche organisation which emerged at the right time as governments are increasingly look to private, civil society actors to carry out the duties they no longer can or never could (Gray 2013). Despite the rather unusual role Independent Diplomat plays in the diplomatic landscape, the organisation has, as Gray (2013) claims, been "normalised" and become "a recognised cog in the diplomatic machine." According to its founder, what makes Independent Diplomat particularly effective is its "manoeuvrability" as a small and independent organisation with the autonomy to decide which clients it takes on and how it performs its work (Ross quoted in Cassauwers 2016).

Challenges

While Independent Diplomat has demonstrated numerous successes and achievements during its relatively short history, the organisation continues to face various challenges.

The organisation sets strict ethical standards on both itself and its clients. While it has stringent rules on how it chooses clients, it cannot guarantee that they will stay committed to the ideals of democracy and human rights once their cause is successful. For instance, in late 2013, the organisation was forced to suspend services to the government of the Republic of South Sudan following reports of widespread violence including extrajudicial and targeted killings (Cassauwers 2016). With the majority of its clients in areas emerging from war or conflict, the organisation will continue to face challenges where a current or potential client fails to meet its strict ethical standards, which could "dent Independent Diplomat's reputation for discernment" (Odone 2012).

Another significant challenge faced by Independent Diplomat, as with most non-profit organisations its size, is access to funding. As noted by its founder, the organisation's mission is to serve clients who are by their nature "poor and marginalised, and cannot afford to pay the fees that would sustain a commercial agency" (Ross 2007: 195–196). Its work can be "difficult to explain", making it challenging to raise money as not all mainstream donors are open to funding the organisation (Ross quoted in Ladek 2015). While Ross aspires to ask all his clients to pay, not all are able to. This means that Independent Diplomat must continually look for diverse external sources of funding. Over time, the organisation has gained support and funding from various foundations and trusts and from the governments of Finland, Liechtenstein, Switzerland, Norway and the United Kingdom.

Another challenge is regarding Independent Diplomat's human resources. Given the niche work its experts do, finding people who are able to carry out this work effectively has proven difficult. As many of Independent Diplomats' staff are former diplomats, Ross notes that it "takes quite a special person to leave an established diplomatic service" to enter a role that is much more sensitive, uncharted and uncertain (Ross quoted in Ladek 2015). However, Independent Diplomat's staff numbers have been increasing year by year, illustrating that the organisation's reputation is continuing to grow.

Conclusion

This case study demonstrates that it is possible for a think tank to play a role in assisting states to negotiate and advocate for their key interests in international forums. Through its expert advice and representation, Independent Diplomat enables states to carry out diplomatic functions at a bilateral and multilateral level. In doing so, Independent Diplomat has enabled states, in particular newly-emerged and emerging states and the least wealthy states, to navigate a highly complex system of international negotiation, directly providing some of the negotiation and representation functions required in diplomacy today.

2 *Indirect Negotiation: Think Tanks as a "School for Diplomats"*

Think tanks can also contribute to the diplomatic function of negotiation indirectly by providing advice and training to officials who are required to negotiate. This can include providing diplomatic training to equip young diplomats with the skillset required to negotiate successfully or further training to hone the skills of established, mid-career and senior diplomats.

There is an established network of organisations that provide diplomatic training in The International Forum on Diplomatic Training: members include universities, non-government organisations and agencies within ministries of foreign affairs. While some of these might not meet the definition of a think tank, many are organisations that aim to influence public policy through independent intellectual inputs including providing training and advice to diplomats: for example the European Academy of Diplomacy, a non-government non-profit diplomatic training academy located in Poland, or the Academia Diplomatica "Andres Bello" which, along with providing diplomatic training to Chile's Ministry of Foreign Affairs, helps the rest of society develop a better comprehension of international relations through its publications and outreach.

Korea National Diplomatic Academy

This case study will focus on the work of the Korea National Diplomatic Academy (KNDA), an organisation that trains Republic of Korea diplomats in the art of negotiation as well as providing research and analysis.

It meets the definition of an organisation that provides independent intellectual products to exert influence on international affairs. It might not fall within the narrowest definitions of a think tank as an organisation located within and funded by the Ministry of Foreign Affairs.

About the Korea National Diplomatic Academy: History, Mission and Activities

KNDA describes its mission as becoming a "world-leading training and education institution for career diplomats" and a "prominent think tank in the area of diplomatic security" (2015). Its dual mission can be explained by its history.

In 1963 the Korean Ministry of Foreign Affairs created a training institution for new diplomatic recruits. This was reorganised in 1976 to incorporate a research function and became the Institute for Foreign Affairs and National Security (IFANS). IFANS was ranked the top think tank in South Korea by a major daily newspaper each year for the last decade.[10]

---

10 Interview with Taehwan Kim, Professor, Korea National Diplomatic Academy, 3 February 2017.

In 2012, IFANS went through another evolution given the government's focus on improving Korea's diplomatic corps. This involved abolishing Korea's traditional rote-based foreign service exam which had been in place for 47 years and had been criticised for "producing unqualified diplomats who lack language skills and other traits such as negotiation abilities and quick judgment" (Kim 2012).

As a result, the current day Korea National Diplomatic Academy (KNDA) was created which has a division for diplomatic training as well as IFANS which continues to conduct the research function of the institution.[11] The historical identity of IFANS as a think tank means that KNDA is understood and accepted as both a think tank and an education institute. There are similar examples such as the Diplomatic Academy of Vietnam and the Clingendael Netherlands Institute of International Affairs discussed further below.

Within Korea, KNDA's work as a think tank and its location within government are not seen as a contradiction in theory as both serve the Korean people and state; when, in practice, there may be dissonance between a researcher's opinion and a particular administration this can be managed either by expressing views that deviate from the administration in scholarly journals or through circulation to a limited circle within government.[12] It was noted that private think tanks are not 100% free due to the pressures of sponsors and finances: by contrast, "we don't have to go out for money from the private sector; we are financially secure".[13]

Korea National Diplomatic Academy and Negotiation Training

This case study focuses on the KNDA's programs to help diplomats, government officials and individuals from the public and private sectors hone their negotiation skills. To fulfil this mandate, KNDA's Department of Education and Training provides education and training to budding diplomats, conducts the Ministry of Foreign Affairs' Diplomatic Competency Assessment and operates

11 Article 3 of the *Korea National Diplomatic Academy Act 2011* sets out the KNDA's duties as educating and training officials from the Ministry of Foreign Affairs, the general public and foreigners as well as contributing to Korea's foreign policy through its research and analysis.

12 Interview with Taehwan Kim, Professor, Korea National Diplomatic Academy, 3 February 2017.

13 Interview with Taehwan Kim, Professor, Korea National Diplomatic Academy, 3 February 2017.

research and academic exchanges with international organisations and partners (Kyung-eun 2015).

KNDA's training programs are designed to equip candidates "to perform efficiently in a competitive global environment" in line with the changing requirements for entry into the Korean foreign service (KNDA 2016). From 2014 onwards, aspiring diplomats have had to go through a three-step process to enter the foreign service, the final stage of which is entry into KNDA where they undergo an intensive year-long Foreign Service Officer Candidate training program. Not all of the 30–40 candidates are selected to become career diplomats, making it a competitive program.[14] Diplomatic negotiation is a key part of this training.

KNDA also provides diplomatic competency assessment for junior and senior-level foreign service officers. Diplomats are observed and assessed on their grasp of essential diplomatic competencies including network building, diplomatic negotiation and crisis management. KNDA prepares diplomats for assessment over a two to three week program of role-plays and simulations. This can occur multiple times in a diplomat's career.[15] KNDA also offers a three-week consular training program.

KNDA's also offers training programs for government and public sector employees other than diplomats, illustrating how in today's global environment individuals other than official diplomats are increasingly required to learn the skills of diplomacy, including negotiation. KNDA's Global Leadership Program brings together around 50 officials of central and local governments as well as public corporation employees for 43 weeks every year to develop their negotiation skills and enhance their knowledge on international affairs. A much shorter, two-week program for the general public, the International Conference and Negotiation Program, focuses on negotiation and conference skills.

Successes

The KNDA has maintained a good reputation throughout its evolutions and reformations. In 2016 it was ranked 68 in the top think tanks worldwide in the *Global Go To Think Tank Index* (McGann 2016). It bills itself as the leading research and training institution of its kind in Korea and the "birthplace for world-class diplomats" (KNDA 2016).

---

14 Interview with Taehwan Kim, Professor, Korea National Diplomatic Academy, 3 February 2017.

15 Interview with Taehwan Kim, Professor, Korea National Diplomatic Academy, 3 February 2017.

In 2013 Chancellor Yun Duk-min claimed that KNDA's greatest accomplishment was "its transition from a system of selecting to a system of training Korean diplomats" (Duk-min Yun quoted in Kim 2013). The abolition of the old exam system is likely to be very popular and may be considered a success on this basis alone.

KDNA hopes that with the new model the next generation of Korean diplomats will be better able to handle the various demands placed upon diplomatic actors in a networked diplomatic environment. While the program is relatively new, feedback is that the trainees have a very good reputation.

The KNDA Foreign Service Officer Candidate training program is designed to prepare candidates to become successful diplomats. Around 90% of candidates are selected to become career diplomats in the Ministry of Foreign Affairs.

Over an intensive 50-week program, courses focus on four fields:

- mission as a civil servant;
- foreign language training;
- knowledge, including international relations, Northeast Asia, international economics and international law;
- diplomatic competency, including skills in communication, networking and negotiation.

Out of these, diplomatic competency is the most challenging for students. Many would already consider themselves skilled at international relations theory and languages, but the courses on diplomatic competency are not something they will have encountered in their lives. Elements such as diplomatic negotiations, crisis management, strategic thinking, communications and public diplomacy are not generally taught in Korean colleges and universities so students are faced with totally new concepts and skills. Feedback from students is that they find training in these areas useful and helpful.

Lecturers are drawn from scholars and career diplomats experience in real negotiations and focus both on theory and practice. Teaching is case-based on diplomatic scenarios and crisis management including at some simulations.[16]

16 Interview with Taehwan Kim, Professor, Korea National Diplomatic Academy, 3 February 2017.

KNDA's growth and expansion is indicative of Korea's growing diplomatic footprint and represents a realisation by the Korean government that effective diplomacy today requires specialised knowledge and a diverse skillset (Kim 2013).

Challenges

As a relatively new program, elements are still evolving; each year new curriculum is introduced into training. While at present some courses need to rely on outside human capital, for example foreign experts delivering intensive teaching, it is hoped that this will be internalised over time.[17]

One challenge is the demand for diplomatic training from other countries:

> We have so many demands from abroad, particularly from developing countries. They ask us to provide custom-made programs for their junior diplomats; these are not just a couple of days or a couple of weeks—it might be asking us to set up a Master's! There are some who think it would be great to launch a Masters's program at the KNDA, at first targeting diplomats from developing countries and in the second stage targeting Korean people.[18]

Other areas of potential growth are in consular training, given the explosion in demand for professional consular services, and in the use of digital tools in diplomacy.[19]

KNDA has the challenge of maintaining its reputation and promoting its work outside Korea when much of its work is in the Korean language. There is interest in being more active in disseminating English-language research outcomes.[20]

KNDA's close links with the Korean government is both a strength and a challenge: it is beneficial in that KNDA receives a steady source of funding and support, but also may place limitations on the institution's activities. Article 4 of the *Korean National Diplomatic Academy Act 2011* provides that the Chancellor

---

17 Interview with Taehwan Kim, Professor, Korea National Diplomatic Academy, 3 February 2017.

18 Interview with Taehwan Kim, Professor, Korea National Diplomatic Academy, 3 February 2017.

19 Interview with Taehwan Kim, Professor, Korea National Diplomatic Academy, 3 February 2017.

20 Interview with Taehwan Kim, Professor, Korea National Diplomatic Academy, 3 February 2017.

will be labelled a State official and appointed by the President of the Republic of Korea and the Ministry is given the authority to appoint foreign service officials as career professors at the KNDA. As its various iterations demonstrate, KNDA has had to readjust its focus and mandate to accommodate the Korean government's changing priorities.

Conclusion

This case study demonstrates that is possible for a think tank indirectly to contribute to the diplomatic function of negotiation through providing training to aspiring diplomats and government officials. The work of KNDA and other diplomatic training academies worldwide illustrates that think tanks can play a role in this area whether they are independent, university-based or affiliated with their governments.

3 *Direct Communication: Think Tanks as a "Charm Offensive"*

Communicating with foreign publics and facilitating communication between states and other entities is one of the primary functions of a diplomat (Bull 2002: 159). With many foreign ministries facing resource constraints and a complex global environment, it is becoming increasingly difficult for official diplomats to perform this function alone. Nowadays, a variety of sub-state and non-state actors are directly involved in communicating with the wider public to advance an agenda or enhance understanding on specific issues.

Think tanks, as entities with often extensive transnational networks, are active in reaching out to foreign as well as domestic audiences to promote understanding and inform about their home countries. Any think tank with a website is communicating with foreign publics to some extent. Some regard it as an important focus of their work to try to explain their country to foreign publics, for example the Carnegie Moscow Center. A number of countries, particularly emerging powers, are investing in public diplomacy including through think tanks; Hall (2012) outlines India's efforts in this area.

The Chinese Association for International Understanding

This case study focuses on the outreach activities of a Chinese think tank, the Chinese Association for International Understanding (CAFIU). As a non-profit organisation under Chinese law, albeit strongly linked with the Chinese government, it fits within the narrow definition of a think tank. It organises visits, exchanges and publications to promote mutual understanding and friendly cooperation between China and other countries.

This case study focuses on CAFIU's public diplomacy activities to illustrate how think tanks can play a direct role in communicating with foreign publics to promote their country and create acceptance at the grassroots level for broader state-level initiatives.

About CAFIU: Mission, History and Activities

Institutions such as CAFIU were created in the midst of China's reform and opening process in the 1980s to build links and understanding to facilitate China's engagement with the outside world (Hu & Zhang 2016). Given China's rise, and the attendant praise as well as concern this engendered, the Chinese government supported the creation of think tanks both to improve policymaking (Shambaugh 2002) and to promote China globally. These institutions have become an important component of China's soft power and public diplomacy efforts.

CAFIU was founded in 1981 as a non-profit organisation with the mandate of "letting the world understand China, and letting China understand the world" (CAFIU 2017). It provides a platform for dialogue and communication to enhance understanding and cooperation between China and other countries. In doing so, it hopes to build a "harmonious world of enduring peace and common prosperity" (CAFIU 2017).

According to Article 3 of its Constitution (CAFIU 2014), CAFIU includes members from all walks of life in China including individuals from government, political parties, social activists, scholars, media, other non-governmental organisations and business people. CAFIU is led by an Executive Council, which is currently made up of more than 150 members led by President Madame Yan Junqi, Vice-Chairwoman of the Standing Committee of the National People's Congress and Chairwoman of the Central Committee of the Chinese Association for Promoting Democracy, one of the 8 non-communist parties in China.[21]

While CAFIU is clearly strongly linked with the Chinese government, it has formal status as a non-profit organisation registered with the Ministry of Civil Affairs and has special consultative status as a non-governmental organisation with the UN Economic and Social Council (ECOSOC). CAFIU runs on a combination of government assistance as well as donations and grants from organisations in China and overseas.

The increasing number of such institutions in China indicates a realisation of the gap that exists between China's image of itself and the international community's image of China, which can only be bridged by the strengthening of people-to-people links and by engaging with foreign publics (Hu & Zhang

21 Email correspondence with Wang Bo, Chinese Association for International Understanding, 8 February 2017.

2016, D'Hooghe 2010: 2, Wang 2011: 5). CAFIU is one of a number of think tanks in China working to counter misunderstandings, address concerns and promote the image of a peace-loving China that embraces its responsibilities as an international actor.

Their activities embody a traditional, state-centric understanding of public diplomacy set by the Chinese Ministry of Foreign Affairs which views public diplomacy as public affairs, that is, enlightening foreign and domestic audiences about China's diplomacy and foreign policy (D'Hooghe 2007: 6). Essentially, this means that institutions such as CAFIU are responsible for advancing a positive image of the country and its government, promoting Chinese culture, and expanding China's influence and voice in the international arena (Creemers 2015). In this way, they are tasked with creating a favourable public opinion environment to make China's rise palatable to the world.

CAFIU and Public Diplomacy

To fulfil its mandate, CAFIU is actively involved in people-to-people and public diplomacy. Its work focuses on areas relating to international relations, economic cooperation, party politics, culture, education, development and poverty alleviation. To this end, CAFIU has cooperative links with various institutions, political groups and international organisations around the world and regularly conducts exchanges, study tours and high-level dialogues. It also supports the Chinese government with its aid and development programs around the world and participates in various United Nations bodies representing China. Additionally, CAFIU publishes a Chinese-English quarterly journal, *International Understanding*, which since 1981 has drawn on contributions from scholars and experts to inform readers of Chinese foreign policy, domestic priorities and people-to-people diplomacy.

A core part of CAFIU's activities is organising exchanges and visits to countries in Europe, Asia and Africa. By conducting meetings, interviews and seminars between Chinese and foreign delegations, CAFIU aims to create the strong people-to-people links which will have flow-on effects on official diplomacy.

As part of its public diplomacy efforts CAFIU has been particularly active in Africa, for example, in establishing livelihood projects which aim to bring real benefits for the African people. At the same time, creating a friendly social environment within African countries is also hoped to improve the image and prospects of Chinese businesses who are increasingly investing in the region.

CAFIU has also been highly engaged with government and civil society groups in Europe to improve relations and the public opinion of China. For example, in December 2012, CAFIU co-organised an international conference on "Europe-China: Role of NGOs" which aimed to enhance linkages between Chinese and European NGOs and demonstrate China's growing pluralistic society. The event saw the participation of more than 200 attendees from Poland, Germany, France, Italy, Ukraine, Latvia and China. Additionally, since 2011 CAFIU has run a "Knowing About China" program where it encourages NGOs, think tanks and media organisations from Central and Eastern European countries to visit China for study tours and exchanges to increase their understanding of China.

One of the CAFIU's public diplomacy initiatives is its Understanding and Cooperation Dialogue which has taken place annually since May 2012. The dialogue is attended by a variety of civil society organisations from Asia, Africa, Europe and America and involves in-depth discussions about politics, economics, development and culture. From CAFIU's perspective, it provides a means to familiarise participants with the concept of the "Chinese dream," on China's economic and social developments and promote China as a peace-loving nation (CAFIU 2009). These activities are very much in line with China's official foreign policy goals.

The CAFIU organises activities for young as well as established leaders. The 2nd China-US-Europe Young Leaders Exchange Program was held in Beijing and Qinghai in September 2015 including 11 young members from China, Germany, Italy, the UK and the US.

In Beijing the group met with a Vice-Minister of the International Department of the Chinese Communist Party's Central Committee and took part in an international seminar on reform, governance and cooperation. They also visited an entrepreneurship and innovation organisation, a youth club and visited Beijing City University for cultural activities including the Beijing Opera, calligraphy, painting, embroidery, sculpture and other traditional Chinese cultural performances given by teachers and students. Homestays with local families were organised to enable them to understand more about China and ordinary Chinese people.

In Qinghai, the participants were received by a Provincial Committee official and took part in a seminar on promoting regional cooperation which focused on the One Belt One Road Initiative. Visits included a sports training centre, private business and mosque. On the last day, the program concluded with a summing-up session where participants shared their views and feelings in an open and frank way and made constructive suggestions on further improving the program (CAFIU 2017).

Successes

Through its international exchanges, CAFIU sees itself as contributing to deepening mutual understanding and building consensus for the benefit of state-to-state interactions (CAFIU 2009). At its best, CAFIU can build relationships of genuine understanding: as stated by the Secretary General of CAFIU, Ni Jian (2016), the "aim to increase international understanding is not to change others' options, but to help them respect ours, especially to truly understand the reason behind our choice of path, so as to reduce mutual suspicion and confrontation, and work towards win-win cooperation."

It is easy to be cynical about such activities, but the interpersonal connections and lived experience of intercultural contact can be very powerful in humanising others and building a foundation for greater understanding.

For the most part, the public diplomacy activities of institutions such as CAFIU have been "conducive to China's image in the world" (D'Hooghe 2007: 10). These institutions have built strong international networks and participated proactively in informal, second track dialogues with their counterparts around the world (Song 2014: 117). CAFIU in particular prides itself on its efforts to engender practical cooperation with other international actors in the areas of poverty alleviation, education and business (Yan 2014).

The Chinese government has realised the value of drawing on the expertise and legitimacy of Chinese think tanks such as CAFIU. Especially where the interests of the public are concerned, the participation of think tanks in public hearings and meetings is recognised as a way of enhancing the supposed transparency of policymaking (Creemers 2015). Likewise, Chinese think tanks have benefitted from their close links to government and are often invited to official meetings and seminars to provide their inputs on pressing issues (Theobald 2013: 73). This suggests that China is developing a more pluralistic society whereby non-state actors are having an influence on Chinese foreign policy. In this sense, Chinese think tanks are contributing to the reform, opening and modernisation of Chinese society which benefits the country's reputation internationally.

Challenges

While the flourishing of Chinese think tanks is a welcome sign, one cannot overlook the fact that their activities are highly constrained by the level of control exercised over them by the Chinese government (Theobald 2013: 72). It is common for government officials to sit on the executive board of major Chinese think tanks and there is regular circulation of individuals from the Communist Party into think tanks and vice versa.

One of the guiding principles of the movement to create think tanks with Chinese characteristics was to "guarantee that all activities in which think tanks engage conform to the Party line, principles and policies, and abide by State laws and regulations" (Creemers 2015). This leaves little room for manoeuvre for think tanks in China, which impacts the credibility of their public diplomacy efforts. For Western observers, the fact that the state controls the message and uses think tanks as messengers to spread an ideal image of China makes some of their activities appear propagandistic (D'Hooghe 2007: 24–25, D'Hooghe 2010: 30). In this sense, Chinese think tanks can be viewed as providing the façade of a flourishing civil society without possessing the ability to critique and provide a check on the activities of government.

That said, there are think tanks in China which are not as heavily scrutinised and are attempting to offer a more open critique of Chinese society (D'Hooghe 2010: 30). Additionally, some Chinese think tanks that are involved in second track diplomacy are fairly vocal about the need to maintain separation from officials in order not to undermine the purpose of dialogue (Theobald 2013: 74). The challenge then is for these institutions to find room to vocalise their criticisms and advocate change within the system in which they operate. For this to happen, the Chinese government will need to relinquish some level of control and address the issues of transparency and credibility which hinder the public diplomacy potential of these organisations (D'Hooghe 2010: 36).

Conclusion

This case study shows that think tanks such as CAFIU can play an active role as diplomatic actors through communication with foreign publics. Their public diplomacy reaches out to foreign publics with the aim of spreading a positive image of China and a benign picture of its rise. Close links to government provide benefits but also challenges the credibility of their activities as genuine civil society actors. This predicament is illustrative of broader contradictions in contemporary Chinese society.

4 *Indirect Communication: Think Tanks as "Personal Trainers"*

As well as communicating directly with foreign publics, there are also think tanks working to help their governments improve the performance of officials involved in public diplomacy. This includes research on the theory and practice of public diplomacy and provision of training and guidance to officials. Think tanks with an active program on public diplomacy include the University of Southern California's Center for Public Diplomacy in the US, the Foreign Policy Centre in the UK or the Lowy Institute for International Policy in Australia.

The Netherlands Institute for International Affairs (Clingendael)

This case study focuses on the activities of the Netherlands Institute of International Relations, generally known as Clingendael, which has a long-standing and influential program to improve the diplomatic communication.

Clingendael falls within the core accepted definition of a think tank as a non-profit organisation which produces research and publications on international affairs as well as operating a diplomatic academy.

About Clingendael: Mission, History and Activities

The Netherlands Institute of International Relations is the premier Dutch think tank focusing on international affairs. Founded in 1983, Clingendael is an independent organisation which describes itself as "academically independent and as such not affiliated with any political, social, or religious movement" (Clingendael 2017).

Structurally, it is divided into two departments, Clingendael Research and Clingendael Academy. Its research focuses on areas such as Europe, international security, conflict management and diplomacy. Research is disseminated through Clingendael Reports, Policy Briefs, opinion pieces, a weekly newsletter as well as its magazine, *International Spectator*. The research department has strong links with the Dutch government, civil society organisations and the media, providing independent advice and a neutral platform for the discussion of international issues.

The Clingendael Academy provides diplomatic training with more than 140 courses for around 2,400 participants from both the Netherlands and abroad each year (Clingendael 2016: 8). Its workshops on diplomatic training, negotiation and conflict mediation are attractive to foreign diplomats drawing participants from countries as diverse as Indonesia, South Africa, Costa Rica, Myanmar and the United Arab Emirates. A key priority of the workshops is to help young and established diplomats hone their communication and representational skills so as to be effective representatives of their home countries. In cooperation with Leiden University, Clingendael organises a MA in International Relations and Diplomacy (Clingendael 2017).

Clingendael and Communication

Clingendael has a variety of projects to contribute to the theory and practice of public diplomacy. Clingendael researchers and staff have been pioneers in improving the theory and understanding of public diplomacy, defined as involving two-way communication between officials and foreign publics which aims for "information-based decision-making" (Gonesh & Melissen 2005: 3). In this conception, public diplomacy should be more than just propaganda, where diplomats project a tailored image of their home country to foreign publics; instead, it should be about "influencing the environment in which opinions are formed and where attitudes take shape" (Gonesh & Melissen 2005: 4). This requires reaching beyond the official level to appeal to the hearts and minds of ordinary individuals in a foreign country, making public diplomacy a highly personal and diverse exercise.

Clingendael also contributes through training officials in communications and public diplomacy. For instance, in November 2005 the Clingendael Diplomatic Studies Programme in collaboration with the Dutch Ministry of Foreign Affairs held a two-day seminar on public diplomacy which brought together experts from around the world to share their experiences and advice on how best to reach out to foreign publics. Many of the participants were senior and mid-career diplomats who provided useful insights into the successes and challenges they faced in public diplomacy.

In another example, in December 2005 Clingendael published a training manual for overseas Dutch diplomatic missions on how to effectively conduct public diplomacy (Gonesh & Melissen 2005: 1). The manual urges diplomats to realise the importance of public diplomacy given their developing role as "international relationship managers" and pushes foreign ministries to assess when and how they communicate with foreign and domestic audiences (Gonesh & Melissen 2005: 5). It provides a detailed plan on how overseas missions can design their public diplomacy strategies, which includes goals they should aim for based on the priorities of the foreign ministry, target groups they should reach out to and various instruments they can draw on to communicate to different audiences to allow different missions to adapt their public diplomacy strategy based on the unique context in which they operate as well as their needs and resources.

In 2016 Clingendael worked with the Asia-Europe Foundation (ASEF) to deliver face-to-face training for 24 Asian and European diplomats as part of the Asia-Europe Public Diplomacy Training Initiative. Participants were diplomats working for Asian and European countries, the European External Action Service and the ASEAN secretariat.

During a tailor-made programme, participants first deepened their knowledge of Asia-Europe relations and public perceptions of Asia and Europe. They were then provided with specialised public diplomacy training on listening, shaping and sending messages.

Key lessons for successful public diplomacy included:

- Know your audience—only then you can shape your message in such a way that it will actually reach your target;
- Know your strengths and weaknesses, what makes your country unique and what message you want to get across;
- Work together with other ministries, agencies and the private sector to formulate a message that resonates with a broader audience.

Skills sessions aimed to provide the practical know-how to formulate, develop and deliver public diplomacy through real-life examples and case studies. Participants also went on a working visit to the communication department of the Dutch Ministry of Foreign Affairs to see how a public diplomacy strategy is developed and implemented in practice.

During the program Clingendael launched the *ASEF Public Diplomacy Handbook, How to Win Hearts and Minds* for the Asia-Europe Foundation to reach a wide audience (Clingendael 2017).

Successes

Clingendael has developed a strong reputation as a think tank working in the diplomatic and international affairs space; in 2017 Clingendael was ranked 22 among non-US top think tanks worldwide (48 in the US and non-US category) and ranked 17 in the top think tanks in Western Europe in the *Global Go To Think Tanks Index* (McGann 2017).

It is very active, with Clingendael's latest Annual Report reporting that in 2015 it organised more than 30 events in Netherlands and overseas, its website attracted 335,659 visits and its research outputs numbered 284 publications. The Clingendael Newsletter garnered more than 4,400 subscribers and the *International Spectator* was distributed to more than 2,550 subscribers (Clingendael 2016: 8).

Clingendael's work on public diplomacy has had impact. Clingendael scholars, including Senior Research Fellow Professor Jan Melissen, have been influential in the growing understanding of public diplomacy. Professor Melissen is founding co-editor of *The Hague Journal of Diplomacy*, the premier research journal for the study of diplomacy and its role in international relations. Clingendael researchers regularly write for expert and non-expert audiences on the conduct of diplomacy and diplomatic communications and are widely-read and cited (Gonesh & Melissen 2005, D'Hooghe 2007 and 2010; Melissen 2013a and 2013b, Okano-Heijmans 2013 and 2016, Huijgh 2016).

Challenges

Despite these successes, Clingendael continues to face various challenges, many of which are common to many think tanks working in this area. One such challenge is the difficulty of keeping up-to-date with rapid changes in the global landscape and staying on top of world events. While Clingendael has specific areas of research, its staff must also be flexible enough to respond to international developments as they arise so that they can produce policy-relevant work and maintain their position of authority in the field. With around 100 employees, the organisation cannot reasonably respond to all international events. To manage this, it often draws on its broader network of fellows, associates, consultants and partner think tanks to cover gaps in knowledge (Clingendael 2016: 6).

Another dilemma for Clingendael is maintaining its international visibility. The institute has close relations with the Dutch ministries of Foreign Affairs and Defence, but is also active on the international playing field and in commercial markets. The majority of its outputs are in English, but Clingendael also needs to cater for an important domestic market. As former director Ko Colijn, now succeeded by Monika Sie Dhian Ho, noted: while Clingendael will continue to encounter challenges given the nature of the work it does, it aims to strengthen its standing through "honest self-assessments, and greater efficiency and innovation" (Clingendael 2016: 7).

Conclusion

As this case study demonstrates, think tanks can play an important role in helping officials to communicate more effectively with foreign publics. Through their advice-giving, publications, conferences and workshops, the work of think tanks such as Clingendael enables diplomats to enhance their communication strategies to meet the challenges of a more complex diplomatic environment. In this way, think tanks indirectly facilitate the communication functions required by 21st century diplomacy.

5 *Direct Information-Gathering: Think Tanks and "Temoignage"*

Information-gathering and reporting are a central part of the role of a diplomat. During the age of limited communication, the diplomat was the primary agent for gathering information in a foreign country and relaying it to the home state for the purposes of policymaking. However, in a world of ready communications and endless flows of information, diplomats do not fulfil this function alone. Not only is it near impossible to keep up with, absorb and sort-through all the available information on an issue, but often it is hard for official diplomats to gain the information needed due to their limited reach and elite status. In this environment think tanks as public institutions with extensive networks are well-placed to gather and report information which may be more timely and more relevant than that available to officials. Where they build up a reputation for accuracy, think tanks can become a highly-trusted source of information, sometimes considered more credible than national governments.

One area where think tanks can particularly contribute is providing information that bears witness ("temoignage"), which Medecins sans Frontieres defines as "simply the act of being willing to speak out about what we see happening in front of us" (Medecins Sans Frontieres 2017). Notable organisations that fulfil this function include Human Rights Watch and Amnesty International, both ranked in the top 50 think tanks in the world in the *Global Go To Think Tanks Index* in 2016 (McGann 2017).

International Crisis Group

This case study considers the work of International Crisis Group, a non-profit organisation that researches and reports on emerging crises to help prevent and resolve deadly conflict.

While the organisation does not tend to use the term think tank and describes itself as "an independent, non-profit, non-governmental organisation", given that it produces field-based research for the purpose of influencing public policy, it can certainly be considered a think tank under the definition used in this article.

About the International Crisis Group: History, Mission and Activities

International Crisis Group is an independent organisation focused on conflict prevention and resolution. The organisation was founded in 1995 as a non-governmental organisation in response to the international community's failure "to anticipate and respond effectively to the tragedies of Somalia, Rwanda and Bosnia" (International Crisis Group 2017). In response, the International Crisis Group seeks to prevent conflict, bring awareness and promote resolution by gathering facts to inform and influence policymakers. With more than 15 years of experience, International Crisis Group is now considered to be "the world's leading non-government source of early warning, analysis and advice to governments and intergovernmental organisations in relation to the prevention of deadly conflict and mass violence" (Evans 2004).

From humble beginnings, the organisation has grown from two staff based in London into a global organisation with around 110 staff based in central offices and directly in the field across five continents. Its major offices are in

Brussels, New York, Washington and London with around 30 field offices in or close to conflict zones. Most of its analysts are located in or near conflict zones and in at-risk countries with the aim to anticipate and predict conflict, bring awareness and contribute to conflict resolution.

International Crisis Group has cemented its reputation as a credible source of information through its pioneering methodology in field research and analysis led by its team of experts. The organisation focuses on issues it sees as deserving of attention regardless of whether they are a priority for any particular government or the international community in general. In this way, it maintains a strong degree of independence in setting its own agenda. In carrying out its functions, International Crisis Group is "unencumbered by ideology, competing national interests or private gain, owing allegiance first and foremost to the facts on the ground" (*International Crisis Group website*). Driven by facts, International Crisis Group seeks to present credible information and analysis of a situation it considers should receive attention from the international community, performing the diplomatic function of information-gathering.

International Crisis Group and Information-Gathering

A core component of International Crisis Group's work is information-gathering and reporting through field-based analysis. All its reports and analysis are grounded in field-based research which makes its work all the more valuable and distinctive. It aims to "get an accurate take on what is happening on the ground" by engaging with all parties and stakeholders in a conflict (Evans 2004). This includes engagement with civilians, members of the government, armed forces, warring parties, regional organisations and intergovernmental organisations. The core aim of its staff members in the field is to "find out what is happening and why, and research, as they do so, the best possible policies to address it" (International Crisis Group 2017). In doing so, its experts seek to "open and promote channels of communication between conflict parties and/or external stakeholders" taking into account the roles and interests of all parties (International Crisis Group 2017).

International Crisis Group's analysts are largely made up of highly experienced former diplomats, staff of non-governmental organisations, journalists and academics. Most of its experts work directly in the field with some based in the Brussels headquarters. Its field-based staff are "steeped in local language and culture, getting dust on their boots, engaged in endless interaction with locals and internationals on the scene" (Evans 2004). The primary duty of its experts is to identify risks to peace, understand what is happening on the ground and the reasons leading to tension. As part of their field work, experts will seek to identify political, social and economic factors leading to tension and identity pathways to resolution. Policy positions are developed in consultation with central and regional offices as well as through consultation with other think tanks, governments, academics and inter-governmental organisations (International Crisis Group 2014). It benefits from a strong online subscriber base, which includes policymakers, journalists, academics, senior officials in inter-governmental organisations and diplomats.

A recent example of the International Crisis Group's successful information-gathering efforts was its Myanmar report published on 15 December 2016, which "revealed the emergence of a game-changing Muslim insurgency" in Rakhine state (International Crisis Group 2016b).

The report provided in-depth analysis of an attack by a foreign-trained group of Rohingya fighters against the Border Guard Police in Rakhine State on 9 October 2016. Its analysis of the attack highlighted how the incident was indicative of a qualitative shift in the nature of violence in the area and how this would have novel implications for Myanmar as a whole.

The information for the report was gathered through a variety of methods including extensive interviews with various groups in Rakhine state conducted by locally-based Crisis Group staff fluent in the local dialect, as well as analysis of messages and conversations on social media and messaging applications such as Whatsapp (International Crisis Group 2016a: 1).

The report provides valuable information on the new rebel group, including its aims and international connections, and a useful analysis of where the Burmese government has gone wrong, as well as recommendations on what it can do to address the issue more effectively.

Although published recently, the report has already made an impact with its findings being disseminated by prominent media sources such as the *Wall Street Journal* and *TIME magazine* (Wall Street Journal 2016; Johnston & Neelakantan 2016).

This illustrates International Crisis group's influence and its reputation as a think tank working to make an impact on policy through its direct information-gathering and reporting efforts.

Successes

Founder of International Crisis Group Gareth Evans believes it has succeeded in three key areas: high-level field based research to gather information and analyse and understand the situation; transformation of facts into policy recommendations; and high-level advocacy with policymakers and senior officials in inter-governmental organisations (Evans 2016).

Its successes are due in large part to its methodological approach of fact-finding field missions. The International Crisis Group's core activity is the production and publication of reports and briefings on conflict zones and areas of tension, as well as opportunities and options for prevention and resolution (Evans 2012). The analytical reports, briefings and op-eds have not only enabled policymakers, diplomats and other key stakeholders to gain a better understanding of the situation but also to identity options for prevention and resolution.

Through its many publications, International Crisis Group has established itself as a leader in the diplomatic space directly contributing to the function of fact-gathering. According to its last annual report released in 2014, the organisation published 56 reports and briefing papers, monthly Crisis Watch bulletins, 400 opinion pieces, memorandums of advice to governments and media material (International Crisis Group 2014). Its published works have reached over 130,000 online subscribers per year and its website receives over two million unique visitors annually (International Crisis Group 2010: 5). It has a wide and esteemed network of followers, with its outputs going directly to policymakers, journalists, academics, senior officials in inter-governmental organisations and diplomats.

A further strength can be located in the organisation's ability to not only gather facts but to also produce original analysis that is often ahead of the curve. A central part of the Crisis Group's impact is its role in "sounding early alarm bells in places where others had missed warning signs" (Noor 2015). It was one of the first to raise concern and recommend action in relation to the 2003–4 crisis in Darfur and the 2007 Ethiopia-Eritrea conflict (Evans, 2016). The organisation's success is further highlighted when considering its role in supporting and advocating for the emerging norm of the 'responsibility to protect' in response to atrocities in Kenya during 2008, Cote d'Ivoire and Libya in 2011 and in response to mass killings in Syria more recently. A key to its influence is its "intense advocacy of positions taken" (Evans 2016).

The international community has become much more willing and more effective than ever before at preventing the outbreak of war and mass violence, and the work of the Crisis Group has undoubtedly contributed to this outcome (Evans 2004). World leaders and governments regard the Crisis Group's inputs as valuable, even if the Crisis Group's outputs may be highly critical of government and not what policymakers always want to hear. For instance, former US Secretary of State General Colin Powell considers that the International Crisis Group is making a valuable contribution to "peace and security, to resolving conflicts, to helping people in desperate need, to ringing the alarm bells of the international community, to be a mirror for the conscience of the world" (Powell quoted in International Crisis Group 2011). The organisation has managed to attract ongoing financial support from more than 20 governments which, as Gareth Evans argues "wouldn't happen if we weren't thought to be useful" (Evans 2004). Its policy influence is undeniable.

Challenges

Despite its successes, International Crisis Group continues to face various challenges. An unavoidable challenge is the security of staff who are located in or near conflict zones. Placing priority on fact-finding missions necessarily places a large number of its staff in precarious security situations. Since fact-finding missions are at the very core of the organisation's activities, its staff must be flexible and willing to work in potentially dangerous situations. Maintaining a physical presence in conflict zones while ensuring the security of its staff has been identified as a key priority for the organisation moving forward.

Another challenge is to build international will to respond to the emerging crises that International Crisis Group identifies. It is able to offer an "early warning" mechanism; however it is international organisations and individual states that need to respond to avoid the crises of which it warns. International Crisis Group is thus constantly facing the challenge of building a constituency of states and/or international organisations to respond to crises as they unfold. Thus, while it may be an authoritative source of information for policymakers and the public, International Crisis Group may not always succeed in getting the issues it deems important on the policy agenda. However, its role in creating awareness and stimulating debate is undeniable.

Conclusion

As this case study demonstrates, think tanks can play a key role in directly gathering facts and information on pertinent issues and reporting to the international community. Through such activities, think tanks directly fulfil the diplomatic functions of information-gathering and reporting at which they are often more successful than official diplomats given their unique position as civil society actors with networks of staff and supporters worldwide.

6 *Indirect Information-Gathering: Think Tanks as "Chief Knowledge Officer"*

As well as contributing directly to information-gathering and reporting, think tanks can indirectly facilitate this diplomatic function in a range of ways. This includes setting policy agendas through the information they provide, as well as training public officials in information-gathering and analysis.

A prominent example is the RAND Corporation which in addition to gathering data helps set the agenda for government policy and trains future public policy experts at its graduate school. Through its activities it helps "policymakers make decisions that are based on the best available information ... [its] results are fueled by the best data, the strongest methods, and the brightest minds."

Fundação Getulio Vargas

This case study considers the work of Brazilian think tank Fundação Getulio Vargas (FGV) and how, through its activities, it has supported information-gathering and policymaking by officials.

FGV describes itself as a think tank, specifically "one of the top 10 think tanks in the world" (FGV 2017). As a non-government, non-profit organisation that produces research to influence public policy, it falls within the core definition of a think tank—although its education activities are unusually extensive and comprehensive.

About the Fundação Getulio Vargas: History, Mission and Activities

Founded in 1944 as a private non-profit foundation, FGV was formed with the aim of providing high quality training to students for a career in administration both within the public and private sectors. Along with its central office located in Rio de Janeiro, FGV also has eight schools and two research institutes. It also operates technical assistance projects and a publishing unit.

Its focus has always been on national development through working with government, as evident in its mission statement to 'stimulate national social and economic development' and 'pursue its broader mission through the improvement of public administration' (FGV 2017).

At its core, FGV is an education provider offering courses at the undergraduate and graduate levels as well as professional certificates focusing on economics, social development, management, law, social sciences and international relations s. According to its President, Carlos Ivan Simonsen Leal, in a developing country like Brazil "it makes sense to have private, non-profit institutions, creating synergies, innovations and tools for improvement" and this is exactly the type of role FGV embodies (FGV Annual Report 2015: 9). Through its academic research, comprehensive studies as well as tailored programs and projects, it provides the foundation and training through which Brazil's leaders can create better policies.

The demand for its courses, especially MBAs, and the technical assistance projects make FGV completely independent from private donations or budgetary resources from the government either at federal, state or municipal level.[22]

FGV and Information-Gathering

Since its inception, FGV has focused on research, innovation and technical assistance in the applied social sciences. The organisation's Brazilian Institute of Economics was founded in 1951 with the 'mission of researching, analysing, producing and disseminating first-rate macroeconomic indexes and applied research in economics, with the potential to enhance public policies or private endeavours within the Brazilian economy, in order to promote the country's economic development and social welfare.' In a single year, the institute has analysed 2.5 million prices, produced over 900,000 statistical series, carried out over 100,000 questionnaires, surveyed over 25,000 companies, published over 432 academic publications by researchers and technical exports and hosted 26 events (FGV 2017). Its graduates have become influential officials with strong skills in information-gathering and reporting for the purposes of national and international policymaking.

Similarly, the organisation's Department of Public Policy Analysis aims to promote applied social research in order to enhance the debate on public policy and the development of the Brazilian state (FGV 2017). Through its activities, it 'promotes transparency by restructuring the relations between the State and society. It works to develop innovative methodologies for the analysis of public policies by extensively employing new technologies, through an interdisciplinary approach of both social sciences and information technology'. A core part of its current work is the organisation's involvement in social network analysis and a visualisation of data about the principal themes of public debate on the web' (FGV 2017). Publications such as *The Them Monitor, Pulse of Brazil* and *Economics on the Net and Social Network Analysis* offer an array of monitoring and visual tools to understand current themes, debates and positions on key issues, such as monitoring in real time what social media users are saying about key topics. Launched in collaboration with the Brazilian government and wider society, these initiatives help set the agenda for gathering information on public policy.

A good example of a project where the FGV's indirect information-gathering and reporting has had an impact on public policy is its work on dengue numbers in Brazil through its Health in Data program. The project aims to

22 Email correspondence with Celso Castro, Dean of the School of Social Sciences, Fundação Getulio Vargas, 23 December 2016.

"consolidate different sources of data to provide qualified information for decision making" (FGV 2015: 35). By providing the raw data on the evolution of the dengue epidemic and its varied impact in different areas of Brazil, the program helps focus the policy agenda, stimulate further information-gathering by government on the issue and in turn, create more effective policy to respond to the epidemic. In addition to this, FGV has facilitated specific projects to respond to the epidemic. For instance, it has connected its researchers with organisations in Brazil's public sector and healthcare system to maintain a system to evaluate the risk of dengue transmission known as the InfoDengue system (FGV 2015: 19). The system gathers data from epidemiology, weather monitors and social networks to create a categorised risk alert system which is then disseminated online as a forecast to the public and produces weekly reports for health authorities. The project, which began in the city of Rio de Janeiro has now spread widely to all 491 municipalities and has enabled the public and government to obtain information about dengue faster to reduce the risk of infection. Therefore, FGV's role in indirectly facilitating this information-gathering and reporting on the dengue epidemic in Brazil has proven beneficial for public welfare and policymaking regarding this issue.

FGV has an ongoing program of research and information-gathering on agroenergy projects in countries in Central America, the Caribbean and on the African continent. At the request of the Ministry of Foreign Affairs, FGV prepared an economic-financial-technical feasibility study for biofuel production in the Republic of Senegal. The study identified potential regions for biofuel projects and selected promising projects for investment from the private sector.

The study assessed the feasibility of introducing biofuels into the Senegal energy matrix and the capacity to attract private investment. It identified key metrics to be monitored, including monetary circulation, remittances and investments in farming equipment and machinery.

FGV is aware of how important the biofuel sector is as a major tool to leverage developing economies and has been making efforts to produce and convey knowledge through the economic-financial-technical feasibility studies for biofuel production, showing its feasibility and effective contribution to reducing poverty in addition to other benefits (FGV 2010).

Successes

As a think tank and provider of higher-education, FGV has achieved numerous successes and milestones. According to the 2015 *Global Go To Think Tanks Index*, FGV ranked number one in think tanks located in Central and South

America, 14 in domestic economic think tanks and 11 in the top international development think tanks (McGann 2017). FGV's activities and role in 'research, analysis and public policy design has earned the institution international recognition as a think tank', contributing to Brazil's reputation in the international sphere (FGV 2017). In relation to facilitating information-gathering, FGV President Carlos Ivan Simonsen Leal makes the bold claim that "FGV introduced Brazil to Brazil" given that through the institution's activities, the "country learned to see itself through numbers, indexes and statistics that spoke of who it was" (FGV 2015: 9).

Its level of output is impressive. As of 2015 FGV had 3592 undergraduate students, 1341 Master's students, 443 PhD students and 499 new graduates (FGV 2015). FGV's undergraduate courses have appeared repeatedly in recent years in the top position in national rankings compiled by the Brazilian Ministry of Education and Culture.[23] Recent figures show that that FGV has published 2854 academic publications and 425 books by professors, researchers and technical experts of FGV. In addition, it has organised and co-organised 657 seminars. According to President Leal, FGV's "primary contribution is to improve the functioning of institutions" in Brazil so as to improve the quality of government (FGV 2015).

Challenges

FGV has encountered challenges similar to its counterparts in other countries. Like many think tanks, FGV has encountered the challenge of balancing quantity and timeliness with quality. The high demand for instant analysis continues to be a significant challenge encountered by think tanks, including FGV.

Another dilemma FGV has encountered is the organisation's ability to continue to remain competitive and stimulate the "social and economic development of the country after so many decades, keeping up with the inevitable change in the structural conditions of the nation" (FGV 2015:11).

FGV has sought to address this challenge in three ways: by increasing and improving its activities; by actively engaging with the public as a 'two-way' road between Brazil's understanding of itself and the world's understanding of Brazil (FGV 2015:11). According to Dean of the School of Social Sciences Celso Castro:

23 Email correspondence with Celso Castro, Dean of the School of Social Sciences, Fundação Getulio Vargas, 23 December 2016.

for the last decade, FGV has also been increasingly present abroad, even though it remains mainly a national or domestic-oriented institution. The Global Go To Think Tanks ranking from the University of Pennsylvania clearly shows that trend. It follows the same trend that made Brazil more prominent in the global scene. For many foreign institutions, FGV is seen as a "gateway" to relevant information on Brazil.[24]

Conclusion

As demonstrated by this case study, think tanks have the ability to contribute indirectly to the diplomatic function of information-gathering through the training of officials and by collaborating with government to set the agenda on issues of priority which require further research, information-gathering and reporting. In this way, think tanks such as FGV indirectly support state actors to carry out their functions and expand their understanding of pertinent issues.

7 *Direct Friendly Relations: Think Tanks as a "Safe Space"*

Preventing the descent into war and violence is the *raison d'être* of diplomacy (Jonsson and Aggestam 2013). As Bull (2002: 164) sees it, "To minimise ... friction and to contain its effects where it takes place, is one of the main functions of diplomacy." In the words of the Vienna Convention, a key aim is "promoting friendly relations."

One of the tasks of diplomats is to ensure that a situation of tension does not devolve into conflict or, preferably, that tension does not emerge in the first place. This involves opening up channels of communication, building understanding and managing the differences within and between states and peoples through dialogue and negotiation in order to create friendly relations in international affairs.

Given the enormity of this task, official state diplomats are able to perform this function in only a limited way, through targeted interactions with other diplomats and the advice they provide to governments. They are often hindered in this task given that, as agents of the state, official diplomats are seen to act on behalf of the state's narrow interests rather than a genuine desire for peace. Hence, minimising friction often requires the skills and resources of other actors who are able to draw parties together, provide the necessary tools and create the space for fruitful interactions.

24 Email correspondence with Celso Castro, Dean of the School of Social Sciences, Fundação Getulio Vargas, 23 December 2016.

As many think tanks are independent, non-partisan organisations, they are seen as credible actors in this regard. Given their status, they are ideally suited to organise dialogues and provide a forum for discussion and debate on sensitive issues, making them effective actors in second track diplomacy.

International Institute for Strategic Studies—Shangri La Dialogue

This case study focuses on the International Institute for Strategic Studies (IISS), a think tank based in the UK which directly contributes to the minimisation of friction between states and other actors. As an independent non-profit organisation producing research and analysis to influence public policy, it falls within the core definition of a think tank.

After examining the mandate and activities of the IISS, this case study will focus on its role in organising dialogues such as the Asia Security Summit, widely known as the Shangri-La Dialogue.

About the International Institute for Strategic Studies: History, Mission and Activities

IISS was established in 1958 in the United Kingdom as an independent entity with the original mandate of contributing to nuclear deterrence and arms control in the Cold War context. In 1959 the organisation published a pioneering assessment of the military capabilities of the NATO and the Soviet Union which has now become an illustrious annual publication assessing the armed forces of nearly all states, titled *The Military Balance.*

Since then, the organisation has grown into a truly global entity with offices in Washington, Singapore, Manama and Bahrain. Its mission has undergone a concomitant expansion whereby IISS seeks to "promote the adoption of sound policies to further global peace and security and maintain civilised international relations" (IISS 2017). According to its Director General and Chief Executive, Dr John Chipman, the IISS is now "the world's leading authority on global conflict and geopolitics" (2016a).

IISS' regional offices organise a variety of public and private summits which bring together high-level government officials, ministers, civil servants, analysts, media and business people to discuss emerging trends that can impact the nature and prospects of military conflict into the future. The aim of these gatherings is to assist in "greater international understanding and conflict avoidance" (IISS 2017).

It is these summits, especially the now well-established IISS Shangri-La Dialogue and the Manama Dialogue in the Middle East, that distinguish the IISS as a think tank that has "filled a niche in the diplomatic market place" by working proactively to promote friendly relations (Chipman 2007).

The Shangri-La Dialogue and Minimising Friction

The Shangri-La Dialogue is an annual meeting organised by the IISS Asia office bringing together defence ministers and military officials from across the Asia-Pacific to discuss the pertinent security and defence issues facing the region.

The Dialogue was initiated in 2002 by the IISS's Director, Dr John Chipman, to address the lack of a regional security forum in Asia which would allow the region's defence officials to gather and "engage in dialogued aimed at building confidence and fostering practical security cooperation" (IISS 2017). The first dialogue, known as the Asia Security Conference, was held in Singapore with the support of the Singapore government and was attended by approximately a dozen deputy ministers and representatives. The next year it saw the participation of chief of defence staff and secretaries of defence ministries. In 2004, the IISS Asia office was opened enabling the IISS to run the dialogue entirely independently.

Each year the attendance list has grown to include the most senior defence officials and the region's top defence ministers as well as prime ministers. The dialogue now takes place every June in Singapore bringing together representatives from over 50 countries. These also include individuals from non-governmental organisations, academia, business and media to prevent a sense of exclusivity and stagnation developing—a key danger for non-official diplomacy (Capie & Taylor 2010: 364; Capie 2010).

The structure of the summit and topics of discussion have remained similar each year. Typically, the summit runs for between 2 to 3 days and begins with a keynote speech given by a head of state of a participating country. The first day is devoted to closed bilateral meetings between defence ministers and other officials providing a valuable opportunity for them to network and put forward their interests and concerns on issues of bilateral significance (Capie & Taylor 2010: 366). Following this, the remainder of the dialogue consists of various formal plenary sessions as well as social gatherings. An early innovation was the use of break-out groups where a smaller number of senior officials gather to discuss specific issues off-the-record enabling more open and targeted communication.

As a defence and security gathering the topics of discussion are primarily about the pressing security issues facing the region at the time but discussions also focus on more global and enduring challenges. For example, in 2011 debate at the dialogue shifted noticeably to address non-traditional security threats and the growing tensions in the South China Sea.

The latest Shangri-La Dialogue took place from 3–5 June 2016 in Singapore, gathering representatives from 52 countries, 600 delegates and 2779 participants in total (Chipman 2016b).

Notable addresses were made by US Secretary of Defence, Ash Carter, on the US's vision for an Asia-Pacific guided by common rules and norms—a "principled security network"; by the Korean Minister of Defence criticising North Korea's nuclear ambitions and calling on the international community to impose tougher sanctions on the regime; and by the Chinese People's Liberation Army Chief of Staff, Admiral Sun Jianguo who highlighted China's role in fostering international peace and security and berated those who still hold a Cold War mentality when it comes to China (Chipman 2016b; Hwai 2016).

Wider themes in the summit focused on the issues of migration, counterterrorism, military competition and cybersecurity (Zheng 2016).

Successes

The Shangri-La Dialogue has now become Asia's leading defence summit and an example of effective defence diplomacy. The event has gone from strength to strength as seen with the growing attendance numbers and stature of attendees at each successive summit.

It has enabled IISS to enhance its standing, with IISS currently ranked 4 worldwide (non-US) in the University of Pennsylvania's *Global Go To Think Tank Index* (McGann 2017). The summit also allowed the IISS to "globalize its role" given that in its early years the institute was criticised for having a Western bias (Capie & Taylor 2010: 361–62). As a result, a similar initiative was launched by the IISS in the Middle East in 2015 named the Manama Dialogue.

According to IISS, the Shangri-La Dialogue is "the most important regular gathering of defence professionals in the region ... a vital annual fixture in the diaries of Asia-Pacific defence ministers and their civilian and military chiefs of staff" (IISS 2008: 7). It has consistently drawn high-level participation from the United States, with Deputy Secretary of Defence Paul Wolfowitz leading delegation at the first summit. The participation of top-level Chinese officials from 2007 was another victory given that for many years China failed to attend fearing that the forum would provide an opportunity for 'China bashing' (Capie & Taylor 2010: 363). The regular participation of Chinese officials since then indicates China's turn towards multilateral forms of engagement in the region so as to be seen as a constructive power (Bisley & Taylor 2015).

In terms of measuring its effectiveness in minimising friction, there are numerous examples of the forum leading to practical security cooperation and consensus on sensitive security issues.

For instance, at the 2004 and 2005 dialogues, consensus was reached on common principles on the role of littoral states and interested outside powers in the Malacca Strait (Koh et al. 2006: 58). At the 2008 dialogue, to address the concern of some states towards the use of unilateral military action in aid delivery, participants agreed to a common set of principles to guide the regional response to humanitarian disasters (Capie & Taylor 2010: 367). In this way, the dialogue has provided a "critical barometer ... to assess both the commitments of key players and the stakes for all in the region and beyond" (IISS 2016).

Its success is due to its receptivity to the priorities and interests of officials in the region. Given that it does not aim to produce any binding agreement for participants to sign up, it allows for more free-flowing and open discussion. As Capie and Taylor (2010: 370) note, "This thin institutionalization seems to be an attractive feature." In enabling the officials gathered to communicate openly with each other on sensitive issues, the Dialogue has engendered a genuine sense of community to develop among them in a relatively short time frame, something which other long-standing dialogues in Asia including ASEAN and the ASEAN Regional Forum have often struggled to achieve (Capie & Taylor 2010: 360). Given these successes, the Shangri-La Dialogue is now touted as one of the top security forums worldwide (Hwai 2016) with the IISS presenting itself as a "key regional strategic actor, helping to develop sound, sustainable policies" (IISS 2016).

Challenges

Despite the successes of the Shangri-La Dialogue, it has been subject to some criticisms and challenges. Firstly, given that the summit was launched by a London-based think tank, the Dialogue has been viewed by some observers in the region as a "Western and European initiative without roots in Asia" (Capie & Taylor 2010: 369). For some, it has unsettled the 'ASEAN way' of doing diplomacy and allowed outside powers to comment on and dictate regional security priorities. However, according to other observers, it indicates the importance other regions place on the Asia-Pacific and the flow-on effects of security issues in the region (Desker 2010: 231).

Additionally, while the summit for the most part engenders genuine dialogue between the region's top defence and security officials, it has at times provided an opportunity for propaganda or pointed attacks on specific countries. For instance, at the 2014 dialogue, US Secretary of Defence Mark Hagel made openly critical comments condemning China's "unilateral actions" in the South China Sea which put the Chinese delegation led by General Wang Guangzhong on the defensive. China, in particular, has often used the forum to repeat an official line, for example at the 2015 summit when the Chinese representative Sun Jianguo determinedly followed the script reiterating China's peaceful intentions and its genuine claims in the South China Sea (Glaser 2015, Dobell 2016). This illustrates the challenges faced by gatherings of this sort to foster more flexible discussions between officials given the constraints they face as senior representatives of their countries.

Most importantly, despite the participation of non-government, civil society actors, the Shangri-La Dialogue has increasingly become a track 1, hierarchical forum structured on the hard-power capabilities of participants (Capie & Taylor 2010: 369). Non-official delegates are often excluded from the majority of the closed-door sessions where much of the genuine dialogue takes place. Hence, there is limited interaction between these individuals and the officials gathered, which brings into question the reach of the forum and its relevance for wider civil society (Capie & Taylor 2010: 365). There is a difficult trade-off between the level of exclusivity necessary for decision-makers to interact and reach a consensus on issues and the desire to provide a conduit for non-government insights and perspectives to reach officials.

Conclusion

This case study shows that think tanks can provide a forum for official discussions which directly contributes to minimising friction and promoting friendly relations between states. Through its dialogues the IISS has fostered greater understanding and open communication between key states which has enabled them to manage tensions and cooperate to address significant security issues.

8 *Indirect Friendly Relations: Think Tanks as "Wise Counsel"*

In addition to minimising friction directly through dialogues, think tanks can also indirectly assist to minimise friction between states and other actors through the provision of analysis and advice.

A core part of the work of most think tanks involved in international relations is to give advice to states on how they can improve the conduct of their foreign policy and diplomacy to promote friendly relations with other states. Think tanks that provide foreign policy advice include the Council on Foreign Relations in the US, Chatham House in the UK, Institut Francais des Relations Internationales in France, Consejo Argentino para las Relaciones Internationales in Argentina, Institute for World Economy and International Relations in Russia, the Centre for International Governance Innovation in Canada, the Polish Institute of International Affairs, the Japan Institute of International Affairs, the China Institute of International Studies, the Singapore Institute of International Affairs and dozens of others.

Out of many options, this case study focuses on a leading African think tank that plays this role, the South African Institute of International Affairs. As an independent non-profit that produces research and analysis to influence public policy, its mandate, activities and structure fall safely into the most common understandings of what a think tank is. While it is located on the campus of the University of the Witswaterand in Johannesburg it is registered as a non-profit under South African law and has an independent governing council (SAIIA 2017).

South African Institute of International Affairs

The South African Institute of International Affairs (SAIIA) has a range of activities which contribute in some way, both indirectly and directly, to all four diplomatic functions. However, this case study looks specifically at SAIIA's role in indirectly contributing to the diplomatic functions of promoting friendly relations and minimising friction in international affairs.

About the South African Institute of International Affairs: History, Mission and Activities

Since its creation in 1934, SAIIA has undergone several transformations in response to domestic and regional political developments. Today, SAIIA is an independent not-for-profit organisation focused on providing local and regional policymakers with original and independent research and policy advice. In addition to building relationships with policymakers, SAIIA has built strong relations with industry leaders and civil society. In its current form, SAIIA is a highly-focused think tank specialising in international relations, regional political and economic relations and the analysis of south-south cooperation.

SAIIA's vision is for a "well-governed, peaceful, economically sustainable and globally engaged Africa" and it aims to be "the pre-eminent think tank on Africa and on global issues as they affect Africa" (SAIIA 2017). To meet this end, SAIIA seeks to contribute to policy development and to promoting dialogue on issues pertinent to Africa in an international context by "undertaking policy research, stimulating informed public debate, and building leadership and research excellence in Africa" (SAIIA 2017).

SAIIA aims to achieve its goal by developing policy-relevant advice, playing an active role in stimulating and engaging debate and building leaders and research excellence in a dynamic global context. SAIIA's peer-reviewed journal, the *South African Journal of International Affairs*, publishes Africa policy-relevant research undertaken external to the institute. Through its work, SAIIA seeks to encourage wider and more informed awareness of international relations, especially as they affect Africa.

SAIIA and Friendly Relations

SAIIA focuses its research efforts on a number of areas of potential friction in international affairs: economic diplomacy; foreign policy; emerging relations between Africa and the rising powers China, India and Brazil; governance and the African Peer Review Mechanism; and the governance of Africa's resources. SAIIA publishes and disseminates its research in a variety of forms including policy briefs, videos, articles workshops and conferences to reach policymakers across the continent and beyond. A core component of research published by the SAIIA concern policy briefings by experts on issues of pertinence to South Africa and the wider African community which are aimed squarely at influencing foreign policy approaches.

A project the SAIIA undertakes which indirectly contributes to minimising friction is its Foreign Policy Programme. The programme focuses on research and events which cover a few core areas relating to: South African foreign policy; the foreign policy of prominent African countries in the region with a focus on regional peace and stability; and the role of external powers in Africa working towards promoting development, peace and security in Africa and beyond.

It aims to "produce a body of work that assists policymakers, the business community and civil society working in the continent (SAIIA 2015: 20). Recent work published by this program includes research on South Africa's role in Africa as a peace-builder, for instance "South Africa's State-Building Role in the DRC: Kicking the Can Down the Road" published on 15 December 2016.

As another example, in December 2015 the Foreign Policy department organised an event with the Overseas Development Institute which focused on China's engagement in Africa, building mutual understanding and trust, and looking at how the region can engage more constructively with China (SAIIA 2015: 22).

The events and research conducted under this program have made a valuable contribution to providing ideas and inputs to South African and regional policymakers on how to avoid conflict and promote better relations between external powers and the African continent as a whole.

Successes

According to its Chief Executive, Elizabeth Sidiropoulous, the SAIIA has "a long and proud history of providing thought leadership in Africa" (Sidiropoulos quoted in SAIIA 2015: 5). Through its work, SAIIA has been highly successful in disseminating ideas to help minimise friction. SAIIA has been voted the best think tank in sub Saharan Africa for five consecutive years from 2009 to 2013 in the *Global Go To Think Tank Index*.

Its *2015 SAIIA Highlights Brochure* highlights the organisation's latest achievements. In terms of broad successes, the SAIIA has achieved closer linkages between SAIIA's research and policy community, implemented a media communications department, launched new areas of research including on emerging powers and Africa, African driver states and global economic governance and Africa, and restructured the organisation to improve operational capacity.

Specifically, in 2015, SAIIA organised 61 events, as well as 3 closed diplomatic briefings, 5 briefings to the media, and a range of seminars, conferences and workshops. Its publication outputs totalled 66 which consisted of 25 policy insights, 24 policy briefs, 15 occasional papers and two research reports. Its online influence and reach also increased with the Institute garnering 3961 followers on Facebook and 4373 followers on Twitter by the end of 2015 (SAIIA 2015: 11, 32, 34).

SAIIA continues to cement its reputation as a powerful convening platform within the region and internationally, bringing together government, business and civil society to discuss issues impacting Africa. In 2015 it received positive feedback from a variety of groups: 20% from NGOs, 14% from government; 11% from the diplomatic corps; 15% from academia; and 9% from business (SAIIA 2015: 35). This outreach and engagement is likely to grow in the years to come.

Challenges

Despites these successes, SAIIA has encountered several challenges. Like many similar organisations, SAIIA faces a lack of diversity in funding options, increased competition, capacity and time constraints, and the challenge of adapting to the growing importance of the internet and social media (Phillips 2016a). SAIIA has focused much of its attention recently on how to address the challenge of effective and targeted dissemination of ideas and to develop a financially sustainable enterprise as noted in SAIIA's current strategic plan (SAIIA 2013).

In a recent address, the SAIIA's National Chairman Fred Phaswana emphasised that there are many challenges continuing to plague the African continent including poverty, corruption and persistent intra-state conflict. This means that organisations such as the SAIIA should be doing more and should pursue their mandates more aggressively:

> our work should agitate for international and domestic policy processes and propositions that take into account the pressing issues of our times" by providing inputs that are "cutting-edge, impartial and ready to challenge and inform policy choices and practice.
>
> PHASWANA 2016

An impressive aspect of SAIIA is its focus on ongoing self-critique, evaluation and improvement. It has developed a strong Monitoring and Evaluation unit which measures the SAIIA's impact and influence on its target audiences. Through this arm of the organisation, the SAIIA hopes to rethink its approach to achieving policy relevance with a "greater outcomes focus" (Phillips 2016a).

Conclusion

As demonstrated by this case study, think tanks have the ability to contribute to the diplomatic functions of promoting friendly relations and minimising friction in international relations indirectly through providing analysis and advice. Through their contribution to policy discussions, public debate and dialogue, the work of think tanks such as SAIIA assist state actors to carry out their functions thus indirectly minimising friction.

9 *Putting it All Together: Think Tanks Performing Multiple Diplomatic Functions*

The eight case studies above illustrate that think tanks have a role in diplomacy and both directly and indirectly perform the core functions required of a diplomat: negotiation, communication, information-gathering and the promoting friendly relations.

In assessing whether think tanks can fulfil the diplomatic functions above, the focus has been on eight ideal types. A final case study is offered to illustrate how think tanks attempt to perform multiple diplomatic functions.

The Australian Institute of International Affairs

The Australian Institute of International Affairs (AIIA), a prominent think tank in the Australian international affairs space, performs many of the diplomatic functions to some extent; however, it does not involve itself in direct diplomatic negotiation or provide structured diplomatic training. Like many think tanks, its focus is on communication and minimising friction with some information-gathering.

This means that as an organisation, the AIIA is working across multiple domains in the attempt to perform multiple roles. The discussion that follows examines the activities of the AIIA and the successes and challenges it faces as a diplomatic knowledge-broker working in the international affairs space.

The Australian Institute of International Affairs: Mission, History and Activities

The AIIA is an independent, non-profit organisation established in 1924, originally as a branch of Chatham House, to promote interest in and understanding of international affairs in Australia. It consists of a number of independent branches, which are located in seven Australian states and territories, and a National Office in Canberra. It is financed by membership; publication royalties; sponsorship and grants, including from the Department of Foreign Affairs and Trade; and tax deductible donations from individuals and organisations.

The AIIA provides a forum for discussion and debate, but does not seek to formulate its own institutional views. Prohibited by its constitution from expressing an opinion on issues in international affairs, it sees its role as providing a forum for debate through events, publications, dialogues and outreach to the community.

The AIIA achieves its mission of promoting interest in and understanding of international affairs in four ways:

- *Providing a forum for debate*: The AIIA arranges lectures, seminars and workshops for its members. These range from intimate discussions to large lectures. More than 200 events are held across the country each year.
- *Disseminating ideas*: Throughout its history the AIIA has been involved in the key debates of international relations through its publications. The AIIA currently publishes the *Australian Journal of International Affairs*, the *Australia in World Affairs* book series and its popular *Australian Out-look* blog.
- *Educating on International Issues*: The AIIA also works to educate the community on international issues. One of the key areas of focus is on youth, including schools program, careers fairs, internships and young professionals networks around the country.
- *Collaborating*: The AIIA collaborates with its sister institutes and other organisations in Australia and overseas, including organising second track dialogues. By maintaining close relationships the AIIA can assure an international view on current affairs, expand its knowledge and project Australia's international image.

Targeting Activities to Stakeholders

The AIIA's activities are designed to meet the needs of various groups interested in international affairs. The AIIA 'family' comprises multiple stakeholders including policymakers, the diplomatic corps, members, contributors, the business community, media, interested public, the global think tank community and students/young professionals. The table below sets out the AIIA's various stakeholder groups and their relationship to the organisation.

TABLE 2 *AIIA stakeholder groups*

Stakeholder group	Relationship to AIIA
AIIA National Executive	The National Executive is the AIIA's governing committee and includes state presidents and representatives from DFAT.
DFAT	Department of Foreign Affairs and Trade is the largest single donor to the AIIA through an annual grant for specific activities.
Policymakers	These are prominent individuals within government who at the forefront of making and influencing Australia's foreign policy.
Diplomatic corps	These are representatives of the various embassies and foreign missions who AIIA partners with for its events.
Fellows	These are individuals the AIIA has honoured for their exceptional contribution to Australia's international relations.
Members and friends	These individuals pay for access to the AIIA's publications and events. This category also includes Friends who have donated or indicated an intention to leave a bequest to the AIIA.
Business community (including corporate sponsors)	These are corporate organisations with an interest in international affairs or accessing the AIIA's networks.
Contributors	These are the academics, experts and emerging scholars who contribute to the AIIA blog and publications.
Media	This includes members of the media who regularly approach AIIA for opinions on international issues and cover events.
Global think tank community	This category includes think tanks within Australia and around the world.
Interested public	These are the people with no professional interest in international affairs who visit the AIIA website, read publications and attend public events.
Students and young professionals	Young people can be involved as interns, volunteers, on young professionals networks, as members and contributors.

Given the varying needs and characteristics of each stakeholder group, the AIIA presents slightly different value propositions to each. A summary of these is illustrated in Figure 3 below.

Each group has varying degrees of influence on the organisation and a unique set of expectations that need to be met. Therefore, the AIIA offers a range of products to each of these groups some of which overlap. For instance, the AIIA's online blog, *Australian Outlook*, which provides high-quality analysis on topical international issues is valued by all stakeholders in the network and attracts more than 29,000 unique visitors per month. Similarly, the AIIA's premier event on Australian foreign policy, its National Conference, which in 2016 attracted more than 380 attendees, gives it wide reach across all stakeholders.

However, for some stakeholders the institute offers tailored activities including: policy roundtables and international dialogues for policymakers; a "Windows to the World" embassy open day series for the diplomatic corps and the interested public; publication of its high-quality journal, the *Australian Journal of International Affairs*, for academics and students; and various programs for students and young professionals with a passion for international affairs.

An important part of the AIIA's role as a knowledge-broker is organising dialogues involving academics, experts and policymakers. Given its reputation as an independent, non-profit organisation, the AIIA is able to provide a forum where individuals can freely exchange ideas and opinions, understand each other's perspectives and in this way canvass innovative solutions to common problems.

For instance, the AIIA holds various invitation-only policy forums as a way of connecting knowledge producers and knowledge consumers. A successful example of this was a forum titled "Going Global: Australia, Brazil, Indonesia, Korea and South Africa in International Affairs" which was jointly organised by five institutes of international affairs. Delegations from Brazil, Indonesia, South Africa and South Korea joined with the AIIA in Jakarta at an event supported by the Konrad Adenauer Foundation. Topics included the responsibilities of regional powers, dealing with major powers, global challenges and building an international system that is accommodating of these countries' needs and priorities. One of the most immediate outcomes of the forum was the establishment of solid networks through personal contacts and dialogue which paved the way for joint activities by the institutes. Furthermore, the ideas presented and discussed at the event were delivered to policymakers and the general public through a book publication.

FIGURE 3 *AIIA stakeholder groups value proposition*

The AIIA also holds a number of bilateral dialogues bringing together a range of actors to discuss complex issues in a more informal environment. For example, in 2016 the AIIA organised the third Indonesia-Australia Dialogue in conjunction with the Department of Foreign Affairs and Trade and the Australia-Indonesia Centre. This is a prime ministerial-presidential initiative to enhance people-to-people links between Indonesia and Australia. Bringing together academics, think tanks, politicians, government officials, businesspeople and media representatives, it was a fruitful event which increased linkages between the two countries and produced practical and innovative recommendations in the areas of science, business, media, education and culture.

Successes

The AIIA received the accolade of being voted the top think tank in South East Asia and the Pacific for three years running in the *Global Go To Think Tanks Index* (McGann 2017).

The AIIA has a number of strengths as a think tank working in the diplomatic space:

- Dissemination of independent analysis of international issues;
- Prestige owing to its long history and track-record;
- Ability to bring awareness and recognition of issues and organisations to a national and global audience;
- Wide reach across Australia with presence in seven state and territories;
- Employer of choice for intelligent and ambitious people seeking to build a career in international relations;
- Access to leading policymakers, experts and researchers in Australia;
- Collaborative links with sister institutes;
- Strong network with close links to government, the diplomatic corps, academia and other think tanks.

The AIIA regularly succeeds in securing speakers and participants of interest from the latter areas through lectures, seminars and workshops that connect policymakers, experts and the general public. Beyond providing a forum for debate, the AIIA has also been successful in establishing and maintaining a network among similar institutions, government and academia in Australia and abroad. For example, it has negotiated website republishing agreements with 12 other institutes of international affairs through its "Global Wire" initiative.

Challenges

There are various obstacles and threats the AIIA faces in maintaining its activities. Some of these will be elaborated below and apply to think tanks in general.

While its wide network allows the AIIA to reach a range of different audiences, there is continued pressure to engage effectively with all stakeholders. As each group is only interested in some part of the AIIA's activities and is typically indifferent to activities undertaken for other audiences, it becomes challenging to sustain the interest of all stakeholders. Thus, as an organisation with limited resources trying to spread itself thinly across multiple audiences, there is a real danger that the AIIA will be viewed as peripheral by most of them.

Another challenge faced by most independent, non-profit think tanks like the AIIA is maintaining economic viability through ensuring future income generation. Currently, the AIIA's main income is revenue from publications, government grants, membership fees and events. It relies heavily on volunteers.

Finally, the issue of think tanks being overlooked by policymakers poses an enduring challenge for think tanks working in international affairs. For the AIIA, despite its engagement with policymakers, it is not easily identifiable whether the institute's activities necessarily translate into policy. It is "hard for a think tank to claim credit for a policy improvement" (Conley Tyler 2015a) which can at times lead to frustration and a feeling of irrelevance.

Conclusion

It is clear from the example of the AIIA, that parts of its work might be defined as diplomacy while others may not. The AIIA is indicative of many other think tanks who may not conceive of themselves primarily as diplomatic actors, but do contribute to diplomatic outcomes.

Implications

The Challenges Think Tanks Face

The case studies outlined above show that think tanks are confronted with obstacles which prevent them from reaching their full potential in contributing to diplomacy. There are a few broad challenges that face many think tanks working in the diplomatic space today. These include, but are not limited to, funding and organisational challenges, credibility issues, the ability to make an impact on policy and the difficulty in bringing parties together given the liminal position of many think tanks. This section will also consider why think tanks are not achieving their potential and provide several operations available to think tanks to improve their contribution to think tank diplomacy.

By their nature, think tanks face several broad challenges often impacting on their ability to reach their potential and key players in the diplomatic field.

First, think tanks operate in an environment of low resources versus high demands. Funding was identified as an issue by many of think tanks in the case studies. Most think tanks face the challenge of meeting demands while coping with lack of resources, given that most do not have guaranteed funding. There is an increased demand for analysis of a wide variety of issues but not necessarily any funding to meet this demand. Organisations with limited resources are often faced with the prospect of trying to spread themselves too thinly across multiple audiences (Conley Tyler 2016). Research shows that in recent times, funding has moved away from long-term funding towards increased support for short term project specific funding (McGann 2016: 11). This change has challenged the way think tanks source funding and their long term financial stability. For today's think tanks, the need to source funding for specific short term projects is a genuine challenge.

Second, and related to funding, is the issue of closeness or distance from policymakers. There is no easy answer to this question and each think tank must make its own decision where to trade off independence and influence.

Closeness to government maximises influence (and assists with funding) while necessitating less independence, for example in agenda-setting. On the other hand, pure independence and distance from policymakers means less influence and thus less ability to influence the issues which the think tank was established to affect. The choices along this spectrum also bring other challenges, such as whether to focus on a national or international audience. There can be ethical challenges working with government (or non-government) clients.

Third, think tanks inevitably occupy a liminal position, that is they are located at the edge of different communities within society seeking to link these with each other. If they do this well, they can become effective bridge institutions and help establish common cause (Lowenthal and Bertucci 2014). However, they are always faced with the spectre of irrelevance and need to work to sustain the interests of their stakeholders (Conley Tyler 2016). They are in danger of being viewed as peripheral and constantly need to advocate their value to multiple communities. For those that report and advocate on the need for action on international issues, they are involved in a never-ending cycle of advocacy: trying to convince states and other actors to take action and to make sure that their insights are not overlooked by policymakers. Those that work in conflict environments need to monitor the safety and security of their staff.

This is a particular issue where think tanks are working in areas of public passion where they face societal pressure. They can receive backlash and scepticism both from elites and from the broader populace. Where they seek to provide a space for debate and dialogue they can be criticised by all sides, especially where they are outsiders and their legitimacy may be questioned.

Finally, think tanks face the challenges common to all organisations, such as new competitors, the need to adapt to new technology, the pressure for speed and a range of management challenges such as staffing, recruitment and quality control. Increased demand for immediate commentary and analysis has increased pressure on think tanks, with the 24/7 cycle of news media and need for instant analysis; however these very demands have also opened a space for media organisations, consulting and advocacy groups to compete with think tanks: "the globalization of ideas and constant technological innovation has empowered individuals in a way that poses a major challenge to established knowledge-based institutions like think tanks and universities" (McGann 2016: 11, 17).

These challenges help explain the finding in the University of Pennsylvania's 2015 Global Go To Think Tank Index Report that there has been a recent decline in the number of think tanks worldwide (McGann 2016). According to his findings, possible reasons include:

- Growing hostility in political and regulatory environments;
- Decreased funding;
- Increase towards short term, project specific funding;
- Inability to adapt to change;
- Increased competition from advocacy organisations, for-profit consulting firms, law firms and media organisations.

Thus, while their inputs are very much valued by policymakers, it is likely that think tanks will find it more difficult to be heard and make an impact on policy in the years to come. They will be required to continually innovate and work harder to inject their inputs at the right time and at the right levels of the policymaking apparatus.

Improving Think Tanks' Contribution

As explored in this paper, think tanks have taken on many functions of diplomacy. Notwithstanding this, think tanks continue to face many challenges largely due to the globalisation of ideas, competition for funding and competition for space in the field. A key question is how can think tanks improve their contribution to diplomacy?

First, it is crucial for think tanks to evaluate their external image, activities, programs and financial stability to locate innovative ways to improve and have greater impact (Conley Tyler 2016). This can include reporting, strategic processes, evaluative surveys and other tools.

Second, they have to focus ruthlessly on the usability of their results. The vast majority of think tanks seek to engage with policy, build stronger ties, influence change and inform the public on policy. To influence the development of more informed policy, think tanks should engage with knowledge producers and knowledge consumers early on in the policymaking process. Where think tanks provide input to policymakers, they must focus on the usability of their results and ensure they develop a communication plan. They must ensure they engage with the agenda of decision makers and understand their needs.

Think tanks must learn to innovate and change according to technological advancements, the public's changing demand for information and financial constraints. For McGann, a "forward thinking think tank should look across sectors for inspiration", including the structures of advocacy and law firms: organisations must be willing to change and innovate to "cultivate advantages" and "think tanks must seize the potential to innovate and adapt and be willing to throw the old rule book out the window" (McGann 2016: 10, 12). Innovation will require think tanks to take risks, engage in issue areas they may not always be familiar with and experiment with tactics and methodology. They will need to continually look for ways to inject new ideas into old policy problems, incorporate thinking from various fields and disciplines and push their staff to look beyond the boundaries of what is possible. Only in this way will they avoid stagnation, continue to have an impact and a role in transforming the future diplomatic landscape.

As demonstrated through the case studies, think tanks have a real potential to engage with and contribute to diplomatic functions. This has enormous potential benefits for the conduct of diplomacy. The challenge for think tank leaders is to make use of this potential despite the difficult environment in which most operate.

It is hoped that this first attempt to focus in depth on think tanks in diplomacy will be a spur to greater attention to and development of this area.

Key Findings

This article has explored whether think tanks have a role in modern diplomacy. Empirical analysis of nine think tanks demonstrates that think tanks can play a significant role.

Using a broad definition of think tanks as institutions working to influence public policy through independent intellectual products, case studies have examined in what ways and how effectively think tanks are contributing to diplomacy.

An eight-part matrix illustrates how think tanks directly and indirectly perform four key diplomatic functions: negotiation, communication, information-gathering and promoting friendly relations.

Case studies show that by providing ideas, engaging in research on important global issues, assessing policies, advising governments, providing education and training, and working on the boundary to bridge the gap between academia and policy, think tanks are providing a valuable public good which is improving policymaking and the practice of diplomacy today.

Admittedly, this analysis is built on specific definitions of think tanks and diplomacy as set out in chapters 1 and 2. It is conceivable that a different definition of these concepts could weaken or undermine these findings. The case studies in the empirical section were intended to provide more of a snapshot of the diverse contribution various think tanks are making in this space rather than a comprehensive study of each think tank and an in-depth evaluation of its activities and impact. For each think tank, the case study focused on one aspect of its work which most suited one of the four diplomatic functions. Furthermore, the information for the case studies was gathered primarily from publicly available resources such as the organisation's website as well as email correspondence and interviews with staff from those think tanks that responded to our attempts to contact them. Thus, it is possible that a further exploration into the workings of each think tank may bring to the fore information which may enhance or detract from the argument.

Nonetheless, what this brief exploration into the relatively under-explored subject of think tank diplomacy has shown is that it is undeniable that think tanks are operating in the diplomatic space and are doing things that have influence on the conduct of diplomacy.

It is important to reflect on this and see how think tanks can become more effective influencers; but to do that we need to accept that they are performing diplomatic functions in some sense.

Areas for Further Research

This research is intended to be a first small step in what could and should become a distinctive area of research in diplomatic studies and the role of non-state actors in international relations. This initial contribution has explored the threshold question of whether think tanks are playing a role in diplomacy. However, further research could be done on the questions of how and why.

More comprehensive empirical studies could be undertaken into a greater range of think tanks working in this area to see how exactly they contribute to diplomacy. These could have a country or regional focus, a specific issue-area focus or be an in-depth look at different types of think tanks.

More work could be done on the theoretical model we have provided. This could involve investigating what would and would not count as examples of think tanks performing various diplomatic functions. This would help make the theory more robust and sophisticated.

Additionally, as difficult as it may be, further research can be done into measuring how effective think tanks are as diplomatic actors. For instance, a useful contribution would be to create a model or framework to test various indicators, such as those proposed by McGann (2016) and CASS (2015). This could be taken further to compare the impact of think tanks with other civil society actors such as NGOs, community organisations, unions, activist groups and many more.

There is further valuable work that can be done. It is hoped that this first attempt to focus on think tanks in diplomacy will be a spur to greater attention and development of this area.

Acknowledgements

The authors acknowledge Australian Institute of International Affairs researchers Jeremy Huai-che Chiang and Xunchao Zhang for their assistance.

Thanks are due to the two anonymous reviewers and Geoffrey Wiseman of the Australian National University's Asia-Pacific College of Diplomacy for their helpful comments. We thank each of the case study organisations for their input and feedback.

References

Abelson, D. (2006), *A Capitol Idea: Think Tanks and US Foreign Policy*, McGill-Queen's University Press, Montreal.

Abelson, D. (2007), 'Any Ideas? Think Tanks and Policy Analysis in Canada', in Dobuzinskis, L., Laycock, D. and Howlett, M. (eds), *Policy Analysis in Canada: The State of the Art*, University of Toronto Press, Toronto, 551–573.

Abelson, D. (2009a), 'Do Think Tanks Matter? Opportunities, Constraints and Incentives for Think Tanks in Canada and the United States', *Global Society*, 14(2), 213–236.

Abelson, D. (2009b), *Do Think Tanks Matter: Assessing the Impact of Public Policy Institutes*, 2nd edn, McGill-Queen's University Press, Montreal.

Abelson, D. (2014), 'Old World, New World: The Evolution and Influence of Foreign Affairs Think-Tanks', *International Affairs*, 90(1), 125–142.

Abelson D. and Lindquist E. (2000), 'Think tanks in North America', in McGann, J. and Weaver, K. (eds.), *Think Tanks and Civil Societies: Catalysts for Ideas and Action*, Transaction Publishers, New Brunswick, NJ, 37–66

Adler-Nissen, R. (2016), 'Diplomatic Agency', in C. Constantinou, P. Sharp, P. Kerr (eds.), *The SAGE Handbook of Diplomacy*, SAGE Publications, London, 92–103.

AFP (2016), 'Rohingya insurgency a "game-changer" for Myanmar: ICG', 15 December 2016, last accessed 18 February 2017, https://au.news.yahoo.com/world/a/33572695/rohingya-insurgency-a-game-changer-for-myanmar/#page1.

Aggestam, K. (2016), 'Diplomatic Mediation', in C. Constantinou, P. Sharp, P. Kerr (eds.), *The SAGE Handbook of Diplomacy*, SAGE Publications, London, 220–230.

Agrawal, N. (2017), 'They've been persecuted by the government for years. Now, some of Myanmar's Rohingya are taking up arms', *Los Angeles Times*, 4 January 2017, last accessed 18 February 2017, http://www.latimes.com/world/asia/la-fg-rohingya-myanmar-armed-group-20170104-story.html.

Al Jazeera (2016a), 'South China Sea: Weapons systems installed on islands', 15 December 2016, last accessed 18 February 2017, http://www.aljazeera.com/news/2016/12/south-china-sea-weapons-systems-installed-islands-161214210323393.html.

Al Jazeera (2016b), 'Evacuation of east Aleppo under way during ceasefire', 16 December 2016, last accessed 18 February 2017, http://www.aljazeera.com/news/2016/12/east-aleppo-civilians-trapped-uncertain-ceasefire-161215034620364.html.

Ambrus, M., Arts, K., Hey, E. and Raulus, H. (2014), 'The Role of "Experts" in International and European Decision-Making Processes: Setting the Scene', in M. Ambrus, K. Arts, E. Hey and H. Raulus (eds), *The Role of Experts in International and European Decision-Making Processes*, Cambridge University Press, Cambridge, 1–16.

Anderson, M. (1993), *The Rise of Modern Diplomacy 1450–1919*, Longman, London.

Arbour, L. (2009), 'Civil Society and Public Interest Diplomacy', Address by Louise Arbour, President and CEO of the International Crisis Group, to Georgetown University at the 28th Annual Trainor Award for Distinction in the Conduct of Diplomacy, Washington, D.C., 30 September.

Aslanov, E. (2010), 'Bringing the best brains together', *Trend News*, 1 June. Available online: http://en.trend.az/azerbaijan/politics/1697270.html.

Avey, P. and Desch, M. (2014), 'What Do Policymakers Want From Us? Results of a Survey of Current and Former Senior National Security Decision Makers', *International Studies Quarterly*, 58(2), 227–246.

Bailes, A.,Dinesen, R., Haukkala, H., Joenniemi, P. and De Spiegeleure, S. (2011), 'The Academia and Foreign Policy Making: Bridging the Gap', Danish Institute for International Studies, DIIS Working Paper, No. 5, 1–52.

BBC (2016), 'South China Sea: Satellite photos 'show weapons' built on islands', 15 December 2016, last accessed 18 February 2017, http://www.bbc.com/news/world-asia-38319253

Berridge, G. and Lloyd, L. (2012), *The Palgrave Macmillan Dictionary of Diplomacy* (Third Edition), Palgrave Macmillan.

Bjola, C. and Holmes, S. (2015), *Digital Diplomacy: Theory and Practice*, Routledge New Diplomacy Studies.

Bjola, C. and Murray, S. (2016), *Secret Diplomacy: Concepts, Contexts and Cases*, Routledge New Diplomacy Studies.

Black, J. (2011), *A History of Diplomacy*, Reaktion Books, London.

Black, E. (2016), 'Could Myanmar's Rakhine State become the next ISIS recruiting ground?', *Southeast Asia Globe*, 15 December 2016, last accessed 18 February 2017, http://sea-globe.com/rakhine-state-radicalisation/.

Bland, B. (2016), 'Beijing installs 'defence' systems on South China Sea islands', *Financial Times*, 15 December 2016, last accessed 18 February 2017, https://www.ft.com/content/3575cd8c-c27d-11e6-81c2-f57d90f6741a.

Brunnstrom, D. (2016), 'China installs weapons systems on artificial islands: U.S. think tank', *Reuters*, 15 December 2016, last accessed 18 February 2017, http://www.reuters.com/article/us-southchinasea-china-arms-exclusive-idUSKBN1431OK.

Bull, H. (2002), *The Anarchical Society: A Study of Order in World Politics*, 3rd edn, Palgrave, New York, 156–177.

Bisley, N. and Taylor, B. (2015), "China's Engagement with Regional Security Multilateralism: The Case of the Shangri-La Dialogue," *Contemporary Southeast Asia: A Journal of International and Strategic Affairs*, 37(1), 29–48.

Byman, D. and Kroenig, M. (2016), 'Reaching Beyond the Ivory Tower: A How To Manual', *Security Studies*, 25(2), 289–319.

Byrne, C., Conley Tyler, M. and Rimmer, S. (2016), 'Introduction: Australian Diplomacy Today', *Australian Journal of International Affairs*, 70(6), 581–589.

Canadian Health Services Research Foundation (CHSRF) (2003), 'The Theory and Practice of Knowledge Brokering in Canada's Health System', Canadian Health Services Research Foundation, Ottawa. Available online: www.chsrf.ca/brokering/pdf/Theory_and_Practice_e.pdf.

Capie, D. (2010), 'When Does Track Two Matter? Structure, Agency and Asian Regionalism. *Review of International Political Economy*, 17(2), 291–318.

Capie, D. and Taylor, B. (2010), 'The Shangri-La Dialogue and the Institutionalisation of Defence Diplomacy in Asia', *The Pacific Review*, 23(3), 359–376.

Cassauwers, T. (2016), 'Interview—Carne Ross', *E-International* Relations, 24 November, last accessed 10 February 2017, http://www.e-ir.info/2016/11/24/interview-carne-ross/.

Center for Strategic and International Studies (2016), Asia Maritime Transparency Initiative, last accessed 18 February 2017, https://amti.csis.org/.

Chemarapally, Y. (2016), 'Another Self Goal: Modi Government and China', *Peoples Democracy*, XL(45), 6 November. Available online: http://peoplesdemocracy.in/2016/0605_pd/another-self-goal-modi-government-and-china.

Chinese Academy of Social Sciences (2015), Think Tank Evaluation Report, Chinese Evaluation Centre for Humanities and Social Sciences, Beijing. Available online: http://lyd.org/wp-content/uploads/2016/01/CASS_Global-think-tank-evaluation-report-1.pdf.

Chinese Association for International Understanding (2009), 'Work Report of the 10th Council Meeting of CAFIU', last accessed 15 October 2016, www.cafiu.org.cn/english/NewsInfo.asp?NewsId=1991.

Chinese Association for International Understanding (2014), 'Constitution of the Chinese Association of International Understanding', Approved by the Plenary Session of the Eleventh Executive Council, 2 April. Available online: www.cafiu.org.cn/english/Column.asp?ColumnId=22.

Chinese Association for International Understanding (2017), CAFIU Website, last accessed 20 February 2017, http://www.cafiu.org.cn/english/Column.asp?ColumnId=14.

Chipman, J. (2007), 'Interview with IISS CEO Chipman', conducted by Roy Mathew, 8 December, https://www.youtube.com/watch?v=3WMrdFgaMpg.

Chipman, J. (2016a), 'The IISS Drives Strategic Thought and Action', 31 May, The International Institute for Strategic Studies, https://www.youtube.com/watch?v=bkBGgfrpQls.

Chipman, J. (2016b), 'The 15th IISS Shangri-La Dialogue Comes to a Close', The International Institute for Strategic Studies, 5 June, last accessed 12 February 2017, https://www.youtube.com/watch?v=D_rOxo2JzYQ.

Clingendael Netherlands Institute of International Affairs (2016), *Clingendael Annual Report 2015*, The Hague, 1–68. Available online: www.clingendael.nl/sites/default/files/Clingendael%20Annual%20Report%202015.pdf.

Clingendael Netherlands Institute of International Affairs (2017), Clingendael Netherlands Institute of International Affairs website, last accessed 20 February 2017, https://www.clingendael.nl/about-us.

Cochrane, L. (2016), 'ASEAN meeting on Rohingya 'genocide' ends with humanitarian access promise', *ABC News*, 20 December 2016, last accessed 18 February 2017, http://www.abc.net.au/news/2016-12-20/asean-meeting-on-rohingyas-secures-humanitarian-access-promise/8133666.

Cohen, R. (2013), 'Diplomacy Through the Ages' in Kerr, P. and Wiseman, G. (eds), *Diplomacy in a Globalizing World: Theories and Practice*, Oxford University Press, New York, 15–30.

Conley Tyler, M. (2015a), 'The Role of Think Tanks in a Fragmenting Global System', *The Interpreter*, 14 January, last accessed 13 April 2016, www.lowyinterpreter.org/post/2015/01/14/The-role-of-think-tanks-in-a-fracturing-global-system.aspx.

Conley Tyler, M (2015b), 'Think Tanks Need Integrity, Not Independence', *The Drum*, 1 October, last accessed 13 April 2016, www.abc.net.au/news/2015-10-01/conley-tyler-think-tanks-need-integrity-not-independence/68167422.

Conley Tyler, M (2015c), 'Scholars, Policymakers and International Affairs: Finding Common Cause', *Australian Journal of International Affairs*, Australian Outlook Reading Room, 12 May 2014, last accessed 13 April 2016, www.internationalaffairs.org.au/australian_outlook/scholars-policymakers-and-international-affairs-finding-common-cause/.

Conley Tyler, M. (2016), "Diversity and Diplomacy", *Australian Journal of International Affairs*, 2016, vol. 70, issue 6, 695–709.

Conley Tyler, M. and Beyerinck, C. (2016), 'Citizen Diplomacy', in C. Constantinou, P. Sharp, P. Kerr (eds.), *The SAGE Handbook of Diplomacy*, SAGE Publications, London, 521–529.

Conley Tyler, M., Blizzard, E. and Crane, B. (2014), 'Is International Affairs Too 'Hard' for Women? Explaining the Missing Women in Australia's International Affairs', *Australian Journal of International Affairs*, vol. 28, issue 2.

Conley Tyler, M., Matthews, R. and Dietrich, C. (2017), "Think Tanks as Knowledge Brokers" in *The Age of Connectivity: ASEM and Beyond*, Konrad Adenaeur Foundation, Singapore, in press.

Conley Tyler, M. and Ramasubramanian, G. (2015), 'Diplomacy Goes Personal: Public Diplomacy and Educational and Cultural Exchange', *Proceedings of the 2013 Fulbright Symposium*, Australian American Fulbright Commission, Canberra, ISBN 978-0-646-92661-2. Available online: www.fulbright.com.au/images/files/publications/Proceedings_13.pdf.

Cooper, A. and Hocking, B. (2000), 'Governments, Non-governmental Organisations and the Re-Calibration of Diplomacy', *Global Society*, 14(3), 361–376.

Cooper, A. (2015), *Diplomatic Afterlives*, Polity Press, Cambridge, UK.

Cooper, A. and Frechette, L. (2008), *Celebrity Diplomacy*, Paradigm Publishers/ Routledge.

Copeland, D. (2009), *Guerrilla Diplomacy: Rethinking International Relations*, Lynne Rienner Publishers, Boulder CO.

Cox, R. (1981), 'Social Forces, States and World Orders: Beyond International Relations Theory', *Millennium: Journal of International Studies*, 10(2), 126–155.

Creemers, R. (ed) (2015), CCP General Office and State Council General Office Opinions concerning Strengthening the Construction of New Types of Think Tanks with Chinese Characteristics, China Copyright and Media, January 20, last accessed 15 October 2016, www.chinacopyrightandmedia.wordpress.com/2015/01/20/ccp-general-office-and-state-council-general-office-opinions-concerning-strengthening-the-construction-of-new-types-of-think-tanks-with-chinese-characteristics/.

Davis, J.H. and Lipton, E. (2016), 'Bob Dole Worked Behind the Scenes on Trump-Taiwan Call', *The New York Times*, 6 December 2016, last accessed 18 February 2017, https://www.nytimes.com/2016/12/06/us/politics/bob-dole-taiwan-lobby-trump.html?_r=0.

Del Rosso, S. (2015), 'Our New Three Rs: Rigor, Relevance, and Readability', *Governance: An International Journal of Policy, Administration, and Institutions*, 28(2), 127–130.

Desker, B. (2010), 'CSCAP: Shaping the Future of the Asian Regional Forum', in D. Ball and K. Guan (eds), *Assessing Track 2 Diplomacy in the Asia-Pacific Region*, Nanyang Technological University, Singapore, 227–239. Available online: http://www.cscap.org/uploads/docs/CSCAP%20Reader/Assessing_Track-2-Diplomacy_Asia-Pac-Region_CSCAP-Reader.pdf.

D'Hooghe, I. (2007), 'The Rise of China's Public Diplomacy', *Clingendael Diplomacy Papers*, no. 12, Netherlands Institute of International Relations, The Hague, 3–38.

D'Hooghe, I. (2010,) 'The Limits of China's Soft Power in Europe: Beijing's Public Diplomacy Puzzle', *Clingendael Diplomacy Papers*, no. 25, Netherlands Institute of International Relations, The Hague, 1–37.

Dobell, G. (2016), 'China Rumbles in the South China Sea', *Australian Outlook*, 9 June, last accessed 16 November 2016, http://www.internationalaffairs.org.au/australian_outlook/china-rumbles-in-the-south-china-sea/.

Domonoske, C. and Katkov, M. (2016), 'Evacuation Of Aleppo Underway As Second Cease-Fire Takes Hold', NPR, 15 December 2016, last accessed 18 February 2017, http://www.npr.org/sections/thetwo-way/2016/12/15/505659925/evacuation-of-aleppo-underway-as-ceasefire-takes-hold.

Dorman, S. (2011), *Inside a U.S. Embassy: Diplomacy at Work*, Third Edition, Potomac Books and American Foreign Service Association.

Drezner, D. (2014), 'Why I'm Not Freaking Out Too Much About the Foreign Funding of American Think Tanks', *The Washington Post*, 8 September, last accessed 15 January 2017, https://www.washingtonpost.com/posteverything/wp/2014/09/08/why-im-not-freaking-out-too-much-about-the-foreign-funding-of-american-think-tanks/?utm_term=.44b85092fc5a.

Drezner, D. (2016), 'What Do We Know About the Independence Of Think Tank Research That We Didn't a Week Ago?' *The Washington Post*, 10 August, last accessed 15 January 2017, https://www.washingtonpost.com/posteverything/wp/2016/08/10/what-do-we-know-about-the-independence-of-think-tank-research-that-we-didnt-a-week-ago/?utm_term=.ce054d6bf56f.

English, J. (2013), 'The Ottawa Convention on Anti-Personnel Landmines', in A. Cooper, J. Heine and R. Thakur (eds.), *The Oxford Handbook of Modern Diplomacy*, Oxford University Press, Oxford, 797–809.

European Council (2016), 'European Council 15/12/2016', 15 December 2016, last accessed 18 February 2017, http://www.consilium.europa.eu/en/meetings/european-council/2016/12/15/.

Evans, G. (2004), 'Conflict Prevention and Resolution: The Role of the International Crisis Group', Address by Gareth Evans, President of International Crisis Group and Foreign Minister of Australia 1988–1996 to New Zealand Institute of International Affairs, 31 August, Wellington, last access 12 February 2017, http://www.gevans.org/speeches.html.

Evans, G. (2012), 'The International Crisis Group: The Role of a Global NGO in Preventing and Resolving Deadly Conflict', presentation as part of the SSPS Centre for Public Policy Challenging Crises Series, 17 May, The University of Melbourne.

Evans, G. (2016), 'The Role of International NGOs: The International Crisis Group as a Case Study', Presentation to the Whitlam Institute/Western Sydney University Law School Conference, *The Architecture of Transnational Governance: The Role of Non-State Actors*, 23 October 2015, Western Sydney University, Sydney.

Fielding-Smith, A. (2014), 'A start-up amid Syria's civil war', *Financial Times*, 2 January 2014, last accessed 18 February 2017, https://webcache.googleusercontent.com/search?q=cache:sN4_4KzR4XUJ:https://www.ft.com/content/03bd04b0-5eb5-11e3-a44c-00144feabdc0+&cd=5&hl=en&ct=clnk&gl=au.

Forman, S. and Segaar, D. (2006), 'New Coalitions for Global Governance: The Changing Dynamics of Multilateralism', *Global Governance*, 12(2), 205–225.

Forsythe, D.P. (2013), 'Human Rights', in A. Cooper, J. Heine and R. Thakur (eds.), *The Oxford Handbook of Modern Diplomacy*, Oxford University Press, Oxford, 658–674.

Frechette, L. (2013), 'Foreword—Diplomacy: Old Trade, New Challenges', in A. Cooper, J. Heine and R. Thakur (eds.), *The Oxford Handbook of Modern Diplomacy*, Oxford University Press, Oxford, xxx–xxxv.

French Ministry of Foreign Affairs and International Development (2017), 'Protecting Interests', *France Diplomatie*, last accessed 18 February 2017: http://www.diplomatie.gouv.fr/en/the-ministry-of-foreign-affairs/external-activities/article/protecting-interests.

Fundação Getulio Vargas (2010), *Biofuel Production in the Republic of Senegal: Stage 1 Feasibility Study. Summary of the Final Report of Stage 1*, November 2010, last accessed 20 February 2017, http://fgvprojetos.fgv.br/publicacao/producao-de-biocombustiveis-na-republica-do-senegal.

Fundação Getulio Vargas (2015), *FGV Annual Report 2015*, Rio Di Janeiro, 11–115. Available online: http://portal.fgv.br/sites/default/files/fgv_-_annual_report_2015.pdf.

Fundação Getulio Vargas (2017), FGV Website, last accessed 20 February 2017, http://portal.fgv.br/en/mission.

Glaser, B. (2015), 'China's Missed Opportunity at the Shangri-la Dialogue', 31 May, last accessed 18 October 2016, www.amti.csis.org/chinas-missed-opportunity-at-the-shangri-la-dialogue/.

Gregory, B. (2014), The Paradox of US Public Diplomacy: Its Rise and "Demise", The Institute for Public Diplomacy and Global Communication, Report no. 1, The George Washington University, 1–26.

Goldberg, S. (2012), Leak Exposes How Heartland Institute Works to Undermine Climate Science', *The Guardian*, 15 February, last viewed 1 February 2017, https://www.theguardian.com/environment/2012/feb/15/leak-exposes-heartland-institute-climate.

Gonesh, A. and Melissen, J. (2005), 'Public Diplomacy: Improving Practice', *Clingendael Diplomacy Papers*, no. 5, Netherlands Institute of International Relations, The Hague, 1–24.

Gould-Davies, N. (2010), 'The Two Worlds of International Relations: Scholars, Practitioners, and Diplomacy', Paper prepared for the 51st Annual Convention of the International Studies Association, New Orleans, 17–20 February. Available online at: http://citation.allacademic.com//meta/p_mla_apa_research_citation/4/1/3/8/3/pages413835/p413835-1.php).

Gray, R. (2013), 'How Carne Ross Created a New Kind of Diplomacy', *Buzzfeed News*, 10 July, last accessed 10 February 2017, https://www.buzzfeed.com/rosiegray/how-carne-ross-created-a-new-kind-of-diplomacy?utm_term=.ix68AGZyDa#.jr8XJRq5yV.

Gregory, B. (2015), 'Mapping Boundaries in Diplomacy's Public Dimension', *The Hague Journal of Diplomacy*, 2015, 1–25.

Grotius, H. (2012), 'Hugo Grotius on the Law of War and Peace', Stephen C. Neff (eds), Cambridge University Press, Cambridge.

Gutbrod, H. (2016), 'Transparency as a One Way Street', in *How Transparent are Think Tanks about Who Funds Them 2016?*', Transparify, 29 June, 1–24.

Gyngell, A. (2008), 'Think Tanks and Foreign Policy', *Perspectives*, Lowy Institute for International Policy, Sydney, 1–11.

Hackwill, R. (2016), 'Rohingya fighters in Myanmar linked to Saudi Arabia and Pakistan reports ICG', *Euronews*, 15 December 2016, last accessed 18 February 2017, http://www.euronews.com/2016/12/14/rohingya-fighters-in-myanmar-linked-to-saudi-arabia-and-pakistan-reports-icg.

Hall, I. (2010), 'The transformation of diplomacy: mysteries, insurgencies and public relations', *International Affairs*, Vol. 86, Issue 1, pp. 247–256.

Hall, I. (2012), 'India's New Public Diplomacy: Soft Power and the Limits of Government Action', *Asian Survey*, vol. 42, issue 6, pp. 1089–1110.

Hargadon, A. (1998) 'Firms as Knowledge Brokers: Lessons in Pursuing Continuous Innovation', *California Management Review*, 40(3), 209–227.

Heine, J. (2008), 'On the Manner of Practising the New Diplomacy', in A. Cooper, B. Hocking and W. Maley (eds), *Global Governance and Diplomacy: World Apart?*, Palgrave Macmillan, London, 271–287.

Heine, J. (2013), 'From Club to Network Diplomacy', in A. Cooper, J. Heine and R. Thakur (eds.), *The Oxford Handbook of Modern Diplomacy*, Oxford University Press, Oxford, 55–69.

Higgott, R. and Stone, D. (1994) 'The limits of Influence: Foreign Policy Think Tanks in Britain and the USA', *Review of International Studies*, 20(1), 15–34.

Hochstetler, K. (2013), 'Civil Society', in A. Cooper, J. Heine and R. Thakur (eds.), *The Oxford Handbook of Modern Diplomacy*, Oxford University Press, Oxford, 176–191.

Hocking, B. (1999), 'Catalytic Diplomacy: Beyond "Newness" and "Decline"', in J. Melissen (ed), *Innovation in Diplomatic Practice*, Macmillan Press Ltd., London, 21–42.

Hocking, B. (2004), 'Privatizing diplomacy?', *International Studies Perspectives*, 5(2), 147–152.

Hocking, B. Melissen, J., Riordan, S. and Sharp, P. (2012), Futures for Diplomacy. Integrative Diplomacy in the 21st Century, Report no. 1, Netherlands Institute of International Affairs, The Hague, 1–79.

Hocking, B. Melissen, J. Riordan, S., Sharp, P. (2013), 'Whither Foreign Ministries in a Post-Western World?', *Clingendael Policy Brief*, no. 20, Netherlands Institute of International Affairs, The Hague, 1–7.

Hu, Z. and Zhang, Y. (2016), 'China and the World in the Perspective of Global New Public Diplomacy', *International Understanding*, 23(1), 12–17.

Huijgh, E. (2016), 'Public Diplomacy', in C. Constantinou, P. Sharp, P. Kerr (eds.), *The SAGE Handbook of Diplomacy*, SAGE Publications, London, 437–450.

Hunt, K. (2016), 'China installs weapons on contested South China Sea islands, report says', CNN, 15 December 2016, last accessed 18 February 2017, http://edition.cnn.com/2016/12/14/asia/south-china-sea-artificial-islands-spratlys-weapon-systems/.

Hwai, L. (2016), '5 highlights of Shangri-La Dialogue 2016', *Straits Times*, 6 June, last accessed 18 October 2016, http://www.straitstimes.com/asia/se-asia/5-highlights-of-shangri-la-dialogue-2016.

Independent Diplomat (2016), *ID Narrative Overview*, provided to authors by Independent Diplomat staff member Thom Woodroofe.

Independent Diplomat (2017), Independent Diplomat website, last accessed 20 February 2017, https://independentdiplomat.org/.

International Crisis Group (2010), *Fifteen Years on the Front Lines*, 1–56. Available online: https://d2071andvipowj.cloudfront.net/fifteen-years-on-the-frontline.pdf.

International Crisis Group (2011), 'About Crisis Group', Youtube video, uploaded 7 December, last accessed 12 February 2017, https://www.youtube.com/watch?v=OIlcZWlqj30.

International Crisis Group (2014), *2014 Annual Report*, 1–23. Available online: https://d2071andvipowj.cloudfront.net/annual-report-2014.pdf.

International Crisis Group (2016a), *Myanmar: A New Muslim Insurgency in Rakhine State*, Report 283, 15 December, last accessed 18 February 2017, https://www.crisisgroup.org/asia/south-east-asia/myanmar/283-myanmar-new-muslim-insurgency-rakhine-state.

International Crisis Group (2016b), 'WSJ: Asia's New Insurgency', Impact Note, 21 December, last accessed 2 February 2017, https://www.crisisgroup.org/asia/south-east-asia/myanmar/asias-new-insurgency.

International Crisis Group (2017), International Crisis Group website, last accessed 20 February 2017, https://www.crisisgroup.org/.

International Institute for Strategic Studies (2008), *The Shangri-La Dialogue 2008 Report*, The 7th IISS Asia Security Summit 30 May–1 June 2008, Singapore, International Institute for Strategic Studies, London.

International Institute for Strategic Studies (2016), The Leading Authority in Global Strategic Debate: Annual Review 2015–2016, last accessed 18 October 2016, www.iissreview.org/.

International Institute for Strategic Studies (2017), IISS website, last accessed 20 February 2017, https://www.iiss.org/.

Jacobs, M. (2016), 'High pressure for low emissions: How civil society created the Paris climate agreement', *IPPR Juncture*, 14 March 2016, last accessed 18 February 2017, http://www.ippr.org/juncture/high-pressure-for-low-emissions-how-civil-society-created-the-paris-climate-agreement.

Jayaram, D. (2012), "Breaking Out of the Greenhouse: Indian Leadership in Times of Environmental Change" in Fratantuono, M.J., Sarcone, D.M. and Colwell, J. Jr. (eds.), *The U.S.-India Relationship: Cross-Sector Collaboration to Promote Sustainable Development*, Strategic Studies Institute and U.S. Army War College Press.

Jian, N. (2016), 'Ideas on Promoting International Understanding', Chinese Association for International Understanding, last accessed 15 October 2016, http://www.cafiu.org.cn/english/NewsInfo.asp?NewsId=2581.

Johnston, T. and Neelakantan, A. (2016), 'The World's Newest Muslim Insurgency is Being Waged in Burma', TIME Magazine, 15 December, last accessed 2 February 2017, http://time.com/4601203/burma-myanmar-muslim-insurgency-rohingya/.

Jones, P. (2015), *Track Two Diplomacy In Theory and Practice*, Stanford University Press, Stanford CA.

Jönsson, C. and Hall, M. (2005), 'The Study of Diplomacy', *Essence of Diplomacy*, Palgrave Macmillan, London, 7–23.

Jönsson, C. and Aggestam, K. (2013), 'Diplomacy and Conflict Resolution', in J. Bercovitch, V. Kremenyuk and W. Zartman (eds), *The SAGE Handbook of Confict Resolution*, SAGE Publications, London, 33–51.

Junqi, Y. (2014), 'Speech Presented at the 11th Executive Council Meeting of CAFIU', last accessed 15 October 2016, www.cafiu.org.cn/english/NewsInfo.asp?NewsId=1993.

Kantar, S. (2017), 'The Rohingya Displacement Crisis That Myanmar Denies Exists', *News Deeply*, 23 January 2017, last accessed 18 February 2017, https://www.newsdeeply.com/refugees/articles/2017/01/23/the-rohingya-displacement-crisis-that-myanmar-denies-exists.

Keck, M. and Sikkink, K. (1999), 'Transnational Advocacy Networks in International and Regional Politics', *International Social Science Journal*, 51(159), 89–101.

Kelley, J. (2010), 'The New Diplomacy: Evolution of a Revolution', *Diplomacy and Statecraft*, 21(2), 286–305.

Kerr, P. and Wiseman, G. (2013), *Diplomacy in a Globalizing World: Theories and Practice*, Oxford University Press, New York.

Kerr, P. and Taylor, B. (2013), "Track-Two Diplomacy in East Asia" in Kerr, P. and Wiseman, G. (eds), *Diplomacy in a Globalizing World: Theories and Practice*, Oxford University Press, New York.

Khanna, P. (2011), 'The New World Order … Really: Mega-Diplomacy', *European View*, 10(2), 153–158.

Kim, S. (2012), 'Diplomatic Academy Prepares for New Ear', *Korea JoongAng Daily*, 25 April, last access 28 October 2016, www.koreajoongangdaily.joins.com/news/article/article.aspx?aid=2951968.

Kim, S. (2013), 'Diplomatic Academy Looks to the Future, Celebrates Its Past', Korea JoongAng Daily, 23 October, last access 17 October 2016, www.koreajoongangdaily.joins.com/news/article/article.aspx?aid=2979238.

Kissinger, H. (1994), *Diplomacy*, Touchstone, New York.

Koh, T., Nor, T. Suyanto, D. and Fallon, W. (2006), 'Advance Maritime Security Cooperation', The 5th Anniversary IISS Asia Security Summit 2–4 June 2006, Singapore, International Institute for Strategic Studies, London, 58–64. Available online: https://www.iiss.org/-/media//silos/shangrila/2006/the-shangri-la-dialogue-2006/05-chapter-5/05-chapter-5.pdf.

Kohlenberg, K. (2015), 'I Was Part of It', *Die Zeit*, No. 52, 23 December, last accessed 10 February 2017, https://independentdiplomat.org/die-zeit-i-was-part-of-it/.

Kopp, H.W. and Gillespie, C.J. (2011), *Career Diplomacy: Life and Work in the U.S. Foreign Service*, Second Edition, Georgetown University Press.

Korea Foundation (2016), Interview with Dr. Jan Melissen, Senior Research Fellow at the Clingendael Institute, *Newsletter*, April, last accessed 12 February 2017, http://enewsletter.kf.or.kr/?menuno=4165.

Korea National Diplomatic Training Academy (2015), Korea National Diplomatic Training Academy website, last accessed 21 December 2016, http://www.knda.go.kr/knda/hmpg/eng/main/HmpgEngMain.do.

Kraft, H. (2000), 'The Autonomy Dilemma of Track Two Diplomacy in Southeast Asia', *Security Dialogue*, 31(3), 343–356.

Krishna, N. 2014, 'Think Tank Effectiveness—An Outsider View', *On Think Tanks*, 1 November, last accessed 30 January 2017, https://onthinktanks.org/articles/think-tank-effectiveness-an-outsider-view/.

Kyung-eun, J. (2015), 'Korean National Diplomatic Academy', *The Keimyung Gazette*, 15 April, last access 17 October 2016, http://gazette.gokmu.com/news/article.html?no=2421.

Ladek, S. (2015), 'Independent Diplomacy With Carne Ross', Terms of Reference, No. 53, 12 January, last accessed 10 February 2017, http://aidpreneur.com/podcast-tor053-interview-with-carne-ross/.

Langhorne, R. (2005), 'The Diplomacy of Non-state Actors', *Diplomacy and Statecraft*, 16(2), 331–339.

Leguey-Feilleux, J. (2009), *The Dynamics of Diplomacy*, Lynne Rienner, Boulder CO.

Leira, H. (2016), 'A Conceptual History of Diplomacy', in C. Constantinou, P. Sharp, P. Kerr (eds.), *The SAGE Handbook of Diplomacy*, SAGE Publications, London, 13–27.

Lewis, S. (2016), 'Myanmar's Rohingya insurgency has links to Saudi, Pakistan—report', *Reuters*, 16 December 2016, last accessed 18 February 2017, http://www.reuters.com/article/us-myanmar-rohingya-idUSKBN1450Y7.

Linklater, A. (1992), 'The Question of the Next Stage in International Relations Theory: A Critical Theoretical Point of View', *Millennium: Journal of International Studies*, 21(1), 77–98.

Lipton, E. and Williams, B. (2016), 'How Think Tanks Amplify Corporate America's Influence', *The New York Times*, 7 August, last accessed 15 January 2017, https://www.nytimes.com/2016/08/08/us/politics/think-tanks-research-and-corporate-lobbying.html?hp&action=click&pgtype=Homepage&clickSource=story-heading&module=first-column-region&region=top-news&WT.nav=top-news.

Lipton, E., Confessore, N. and Williams, B. (2016), 'Think Tank Scholar or Corporate Consultant? It Depends on the Day', *The New York Times*, 8 August, last accessed 15 January 2017, https://www.nytimes.com/2016/08/09/us/politics/think-tank-scholars-corporate-consultants.html.

Longhini, A. (2015), 'Institutionalization of Foreign Policy Think Tanks in Italy and in the UK: An Explanatory Framework', *Central European Journal of Public Policy*, 9(2), 96–120.

Lourdes Viray, P. (2016), 'Satellite photos show China weapons in South China Sea', *The Philippines Star*, 15 December 2016, last accessed 18 February 2017, http://www.philstar.com/headlines/2016/12/15/1653717/satellite-photos-show-china-weapons-south-china-sea.

Lowenthal, A. and Bertucci, M. (eds) (2014), *Scholars, Policymakers, and International Affairs: Finding Common Cause*, Johns Hopkins Press, Baltimore.

McGann, J. (2007), *Think Tanks and Policy Advice in the United States: Academics, Advisors and Advocates*, Routledge, Abingdon.

McGann, J. (2016), *2015 Global Go To Think Tank Index Report*, Think Tanks and Civil Societies Program, University of Pennsylvania, Paper 10. Available at: www.repository.upenn.edu/think_tanks/10/?utm_source=repository.upenn.edu%2Fthink_tanks%2F10&utm_medium=PDF&utm_campaign=PDFCoverPages.

McGann, J. (2017), *2016 Global Go To Think Tank Index Report*, Think Tanks and Civil Societies Program, University of Pennsylvania, 26 January 2017, last accessed 20 February 2017, http://repository.upenn.edu/cgi/viewcontent.cgi?article=1011&context=think_tanks.

McKinley Corbo, I. (2017), 'Devastating Cruelty', Vice News, 7 February 2017, last accessed 18 February 2017, https://news.vice.com/story/myanmars-brutal-treatment-of-rohingya-muslims-back-in-spotlight-after-two-damning-new-reports.

Malone, D. (2013), 'The Modern Diplomatic Mission', in A. Cooper, J. Heine and R. Thakur (eds), *The Oxford Handbook of Modern Diplomacy*, Oxford University Press, Oxford, 122–141.

Manfredi, J.L. (2014), 'Los cuatro idiomas del think tank', *Real Instituto Elcano*, 24 September 2014, http://www.blog.rielcano.org/los-cuatro-idiomasdel-think-tank/, cited in Manfredi-Sanchez, J., Sanchez-Giménez, J. and Pizarro-Miranda, J. (2015), 'Structural Analysis to Measure the Influence of Think Tank Networks in the Digital Age', *The Hague Journal of Diplomacy*, 10(4), 363–395.

Medecins Sans Frontieres (2017), 'We Speak Out', last accessed 20 February 2017, https://www.msf.org.uk/advocacy-and-temoignage.

Medvetz, T. (2008), *Think Tanks as an Emergent Field*, The Social Science Research Council. New York, 1–10.

Melissen, J. (2013a), 'Public Diplomacy', in P. Kerr and G. Wiseman (eds), *Diplomacy in a Globalizing World: Theories and Practices*, Oxford University Press, New York: 192–208.

Melissen, J. (2013b), 'Public Diplomacy', in A. Cooper, J. Heine and R. Thakur (eds.), *The Oxford Handbook of Modern Diplomacy*, Oxford University Press, Oxford, 436–452.

Mendizabal, E. (2011), 'Think Tanks: Research Findings and Some Common Challenges', *On Think Tanks*, 2 June, last accessed 30 January 2017, https://onthinktanks.org/articles/think-tanks-research-findings-and-some-common-challenges/.

Mendizabal, E. (2014), 'What is a Think Tank? Defining the Boundaries of the Label', *On Think Tanks*, 22 October, last accessed 30 January 2017, https://onthinktanks.org/articles/what-is-a-think-tank-defining-the-boundaries-of-the-label/.

Monibot, G. (2013), 'Heard a Think Tank on the BBC? You Haven't Hear the Whole Story', *The Guardian*, 30 November, last viewed 1 February 2017, https://www.theguardian.com/commentisfree/2013/nov/29/thinktank-bbc-smoking-big-tobacco.

Montville, J. (1991), 'Transnationalism and the Role of Track-Two Diplomacy', in W. Thompson and K. Jensen (eds.), *Approaches to Peace: An Intellectual Map*, United States Institute of Peace, Washington DC, 255–269.

Montville, J. (2009), 'Track Two Diplomacy: The Work of Healing History', *The Whitehead Journal of Diplomacy and International Relations*, 7(2), 15–25.

Morocco World News (2012), "Rabat hosts the First Meeting on Non-Governmental Diplomacy", 21 July. Available online: https://www.moroccoworldnews.com/2012/07/48915/rabat-hosts-the-first-meeting-on-non-governmental-diplomacy/.

Murdoch, L. (2016), 'Myanmar Army accused of ethnic cleansing as Rohingya conflict escalates', *The Sydney Morning Herald*, 20 December 2016, last accessed 18 February 2017, http://www.smh.com.au/world/myanmar-army-accused-of-ethnic-cleansing-as-rohingya-conflict-escalates-20161219-gte1b9.html.

Neumann, I. (2008), 'The Body of the Diplomat', *European Journal of International Relations*, 14(4), 671–695.

Neumann, I. (2012), *At Home with the Diplomats: Inside a European Foreign Ministry*, Cornell University Press, Ithaca.

Odone, C. (2012), 'Can You Save Diplomacy From Itself', *Foreign Policy*, 26 November, last accessed 10 February 2017, http://foreignpolicy.com/2012/11/26/can-you-save-diplomacy-from-itself/.

Office of the High Commissioner for Human Rights (OHCHR) of the United Nations (2017), *Report of OHCHR mission to Bangladesh: Interviews with Rohingyas fleeing from Myanmar since 9 October 2016*, Flash Report, 3 February 2017, last access 18 February 2017, http://www.ohchr.org/Documents/Countries/MM/FlashReport3Feb2017.pdf.

Okano-Heijmans, M. (2013), 'Consular Diplomacy', in A. Cooper, J. Heine and R. Thakur (eds.), *The Oxford Handbook of Modern Diplomacy*, Oxford University Press, Oxford, 473–492.

Okano-Heijmans, M. (2016), 'Economic Diplomacy', in C. Constantinou, P. Sharp, P. Kerr (eds.), *The SAGE Handbook of Diplomacy*, SAGE Publications, London, 552–563.

Page, J. (2016), 'China Installs Weapons in South China Sea, Satellites Show', *The Wall Street Journal*, 15 December 2016, last accessed 18 February 2017, https://www.wsj.com/articles/china-installs-weapons-in-south-china-sea-satellites-show-1481771066.

Parmar, I. (2004), *Think Tanks and Power in Foreign Policy*, Palgrave Macmillan, New York.

Patil, S. (2015), "China's 'think tank' culture", Gateway House blog, 28 May. Available online: http://www.gatewayhouse.in/chinas-think-tank-culture/.

Phaswana, F. (2016), '2016 Address by SAIIA National Chairman, Mr Fred T Phaswana', South African Institute of International Affairs, Cape Town, 18 February, last accessed 19 February 2017, http://www.saiia.org.za/news/2016-address-by-saiia-national-chairman-mr-fred-t-phaswana.

Phillips, T. (2016a), 'Monitoring, Evaluation and Learning in a South African Think Tank', *On Think Tanks*, 6 October, last accessed 19 February 2017, https://onthinktanks.org/articles/monitoring-evaluation-and-learning-in-a-south-african-think-tank/.

Phillips, T. (2016b), 'Images show 'significant' Chinese weapons systems in South China Sea', *The Guardian*, 15 December 2016, last accessed 18 February 2017, https://www.theguardian.com/world/2016/dec/15/images-show-significant-chinese-weapons-systems-in-south-china-sea.

Poole, A. (2017), 'UN report: Myanmar's Rohingya Muslims face ongoing violence', *World*, 10 February 2017, last accessed 18 February 2017, https://world.wng.org/2017/02/un_report_myanmar_s_rohingya_muslims_face_ongoing_violence.

Rana, K. (2011), *21st Century Diplomacy: A Practitioner's Guide*, Continuum, London.

Renaud, F. (2011), *Les Diplomates*, Nouveau Monde, Paris.

Rich, A. (2005), *Think Tanks, Public Policy, and the Politics of Expertise*, Cambridge University Press, Cambridge.

Rinke, A. (2015), 'Merkel suggests China resolve South China Sea row in courts', *Reuters*, 29 October 2015, last accessed 18 February 2017, http://www.reuters.com/article/southchinasea-china-germany-idUSL8N12T2WQ20151029.

Ross, A. (2015), 'Twenty-first Century Statecraft', in A. Sandre (ed) *Digital Diplomacy: Conversations on Innovation in Foreign Policy*, Rowman and Littlefield Publishers, Maryland, 3–16.

Ross, C. (2016), *Crises in World Politics: Independent Diplomat: Dispatches from an Unaccountable Elite*, Cornell University Press, Ithaca.

Sandre, A. (ed) (2015), *Digital Diplomacy: Conversations on Innovation in Foreign Policy*, Rowman and Littlefield Publishers, Maryland.

Schreer, B. (2015), 'China's 'great wall of sand': calling a spade a spade', *ASPI Strategist*, 29 April 2015, last accessed 18 February 2017, https://www.aspistrategist.org.au/chinas-great-wall-of-sand-in-the-south-china-sea/.

Seib, P. (2012), *Real-Time Diplomacy; Politics and Power in the Social Media Era*, Palgrave Macmillan, New York.

Sending, O., Pouliot, V. and Neumann, I. (2011), 'The Future of Diplomacy: Changing Practices, Evolving Relationships', *International Journal*, 66(3), 527–542.

Shambaugh, D. (2002), 'China's International Relations Think Tanks', *The China Quarterly*, 171, 575–596.

Sharp, P. (1997), 'Who Needs Diplomats? The Problems of Diplomatic Representation', *International Journal*, 52(4): 609–634.

Shergold, P (2005), 'Book Launch at Annual Symposium', Dialogue [Academy of the Social Sciences], 24(3), 1–3.

Smith, J. (1991), *The Idea Brokers: Think Tanks and the Rise of the New Policy Elite*, The Free Press, New York.

Sofer, S. (1988), 'Old and New Diplomacy: A Debate Revisited', *Review of International Studies*, 14(3), 195–211.

Song, L. 2014, 'China's Public Diplomacy Toward Visegrad Countries: Beyond Economic Influence?', in A. Szunomár (ed), *Chinese Investments and Engagement in Visegrad Countries: Myth or Reality?*, Institute of World Economics, Budapest, 108–126. Available at: www.real.mtak.hu/18734/1/Chinese_investments_and_financial_engagement_in_Visegrad_countries_u_150652.439154.pdf#page=109.

South African Institute of International Affairs (2013), *South African Institute of International Affairs Strategic Plan 2013–17*, last accessed 20 February 2017, https://www.saiia.org.za/general-publications/515-saiia-strategic-plan-2013-2017/file.

South African Institute of International Affairs (2015), *2015 SAIIA Highlights Brochure*. Available online at: http://www.saiia.org.za/general-publications/1082-saiia-highlights-2015/file.

South African Institute of International Affairs (2017), SAIIA website, last accessed 20 February 2016, http://www.saiia.org.za.

Stein, J. (ed) (2011), *Diplomacy in the Digital Age: Essays in Honour of Ambassador Allan Gotlieb*, McClelland and Stewart, Toronto.

Steen, J. (2010), 'What Motivates Knowledge Brokers', The Discipline of Innovation. Available at: http://timkastelle.org/blog/2010/04/what-motivates-knowledge-brokers/.

Stone, D. (1996a), *Capturing the Political Imagination: Think Tanks and the Policy Process*, Frank Cass and Co. Ltd, Oxon.

Stone, D. (1996b), 'A Think Tank in Evolution or Decline? The Australian Institute of International Affairs in Comparative Perspective', *Australian Journal of International Affairs*, 50(2), 117–136.

Stone, D. (2000), 'Private authority, scholarly legitimacy and political credibility: think tanks and informal diplomacy', in Higgott, R., Underhill, G., and Bieler, A. (eds.) *Non-state Actors and Authority in the Global System*, Routledge, London.

Stone, D. (2005), 'Think Tanks and Policy Advice in Countries in Transition', paper prepared for the Asian Development Bank Institute Symposium, "How to Strengthen Policy-Oriented Research and Training In Vietnam", 31 August, Hanoi, 1–21.

Stone, D. (2007), 'Recycling Bins, Garbage Cans or Think Tanks?: Three Myths Regarding Policy Analysis Institutes', 85(2), 259–278.

Stone, D., Denham, A. and Garnett, M. (1998), *Think Tanks Across Nations: a Comparative Approach*, Manchester University Press, Manchester.

Stone, D. and Denham, A. (eds) (2004), *Think Tank Traditions: Policy Research and the Politics of Ideas*, Manchester University Press, Manchester.

Thakur, R. (2013), 'A Balance of Interests', in A. Cooper, J. Heine, and R. Thakur (eds), *Oxford Handbook of Modern Diplomacy*, Oxford University Press, Oxford, 70–90.

The New York Times (2016), 'Dole's Role in Trump-Taiwan Relationship', *The New York Times*, 6 December 2016, last accessed 18 February 2017, https://www.nytimes.com/interactive/2016/12/06/us/politics/document-bob-dole-lobbying-documents.html.

Theobald, O. (2013), 'Strengthening Australia-China Relations with Track II diplomacy', *Emerging Scholars*, The Australian Institute of International Affairs, Canberra, 65–80.

Tsai, C.H. (2012), 'International Political Communication in Global Civil Society: A Case Study of Taiwan's Participation in UN Specialized Agencies', *Prospect Journal*, 111–147.

Ukrainian Think Tank Liaison Office in Brussels (2016), "Bruegel Discussion: Why Think Tanks Matter to Policy Makers and the Public?". Available online: https://ukraine-office.eu/en/bruegel-discussion-why-think-tanks-matter-to-policy-makers-and-the-public/.

Wall Street Journal (2016), 'Asia's New Insurgency', 19 December, last accessed 2 February 2017, https://www.wsj.com/articles/asias-new-insurgency-1482192636.

Walsh, E. (2015), 'Think Tank Diplomacy', *The Diplomat*, 7 September. Available at http://thediplomat.com/2011/09/think-tank-diplomacy/.

Wang, J. (2011), 'Introduction: China's Search of Soft Power', in J. Wang (ed), *Soft Power in China: Public Diplomacy through Communication*, Palgrave Macmillan, New York, 1–18.

Wang, L.L. (2013), "Development of Think Tanks and Promotion of Public Diplomacy in China". Available online: http://news.china.com.cn/world/2013-12/19/content_30948444_2.htm.

Wedel, J. (2009), *Shadow Elite: How the World's New Power Brokers Undermine Democracy*, Basic Books, Philadelphia.

Wedel, J. (2010), 'Shadow Elite: How the Study of Post-Communist Societies Illuminates US Power Structures', *Anthropology News*, 51(2), 27.

Wedel, J. (2011), 'Beyond Conflict of Interests: Shadow Elites and the Challenge to Democracy and the Free Market', *Polish Sociological Review*, 174(2), 149–165.

Weisbrode, K. (2014), 'Creative Innovation in Diplomacy', *Diplomatic Courier*, January 9, last accessed 4 May 2015, www.diplomaticourier.com/2014/01/09/creative-innovation-in-diplomacy/.

Wendt, A. (1992), 'Anarchy is What States Make of It: The Social Construction of Power Politics', *International Organisation*, 46(2), 391–425.

Wendt, A. (1995), 'Constructing International Politics', *International Security*, 20(1), 71–81.

Wheeler, M. (2016), 'Celebrity Diplomacy', in C. Constantinou, P. Sharp, P. Kerr (eds.), *The SAGE Handbook of Diplomacy*, SAGE Publications, London, 530–539.

Wiarda, H. (2014), 'Think Tanks and Foreign Policy', in *On the Boundaries: When International Relations, Comparative Politics, and Foreign Policy Meet*, University Press of America Inc., Maryland, 271–299.

Wiseman, G. (1999), '"Polylateralism" and New Modes of Global Dialogue', Discussion Papers No. 59, Leicester Diplomatic Studies Programme, Leicester, 36–57.

Wiseman, G. (2005), 'Pax Americana: Bumping into Diplomatic Culture', *International Studies Perspectives*, volume 6, issue 4, 409–430.

Wiseman, G. (2010), '"Polylateralism": Diplomacy's Third Dimension", *Public Diplomacy Magazine*, Summer 2010, 24–39.

Wiseman, G. (2011), 'Distinctive Characteristics of American Diplomacy', *The Hague Journal of Diplomacy*, 2011, volume 6, 235–259.

Wiseman, G. and Sharp, P. (2017), 'Diplomacy' in Devetak, R., Percy, S and George, J. (eds.), *An Introduction to International Relations*, Cambridge, UK: Cambridge University Press.

Woolcott, R. (2007), *Undiplomatic Activities*, Scribe, Melbourne.

World Breaking News (2016), 'Why is Aleppo being evacuated, how many children have been rescued, where is the Syrian city and why has it been bombed?', *World Breaking News*, 16 December 2016, last accessed 18 February 2017, https://m.wbnews.info/2016/12/why-is-aleppo-being-evacuated-how-many-children-have-been-rescued-where-is-the-syrian-city-and-why-has-it-been-bombed/.

Wright, O. (2016), 'EU referendum: Think-tanks conducting 'independent' research to support Brexit have close links to Vote Leave', Independent, 24 February 2016, last accessed 18 February 2017, http://www.independent.co.uk/news/uk/politics/eu-referendum-think-tanks-carrying-out-independent-research-to-support-brexit-have-close-links-to-a6866011.html.

Wroe, D. (2016), 'Julie Bishop accuses China of fuelling 'tension and mistrust' by weaponising artificial islands', *The Sydney Morning Herald*, 15 December 2016, last accessed 18 February 2017, http://www.smh.com.au/federal-politics/political-news/julie-bishop-accuses-china-of-fuelling-tension-and-mistrust-by-weaponising-artifi cial-islands-20161215-gtbruo.html.

Xinhua (2016), 'China says deployment of defensive facilities on South China Sea islands legitimate', *Xinhua*, 15 December 2016, last accessed 18 February 2017, http://news.xinhuanet.com/english/2016-12/15/c_135908576.htm.

Ying, X.P. (2015), "Development of Chinese think-tank and promoting the construction of national governance modernization", *International Journal of Science Commerce and Humanities*, 3(6), 18–24.

Yang, A.H., Chen, I.T.Y. and Poong, H.L. (2015), "Reconfiguring Social Capital in the Making of Track II Diplomacy: A Case Study of the Taipei-Seoul Forum", *Issues and Studies*, 51(4), 143–172.

Zhao, A.A., "Past Diplomacy in East Asia: From Tributary Relations to Cold War Rivalry" in Kerr, P. and Wiseman, G. (eds), *Diplomacy in a Globalizing World: Theories and Practice*, Oxford University Press, New York, 31–47.

Zheng L. (2016), 'What is the Shangri-La Dialogue and Why Is It So Important?, South China Morning Post, 3 June, last accessed 17 October 2016, http://www.scmp.com/news/china/diplomacy-defence/article/1963157/what-shangri-la-dialogue-and-why-it-so-important.

www.ingramcontent.com/pod-product-compliance
Lightning Source LLC
Chambersburg PA
CBHW071355230926
51846CB00002B/560
9789004331204